150 GREAT
SCIENCE
EXPERIMENTS

150 GREAT SCIENCE EXPERIMENTS

Ingenious, easy-to-do projects explore and explain
the wonders of science and technology

General Editor: Rasha Elsaeed

Consulting Editor: Chris Oxlade

HERMES
HOUSE

CONTENTS

Science at Home   6

Our Restless Earth

Spinning planet   10
Phases of the Moon   12
The rise and fall of tides   14
Ocean waves and currents   16
Changing coastlines   18
Water on the move   20
Cloud and rain   22
What is humidity?   24
The way the wind blows   26
Recording weather   28
Broken Earth   30
Restless Earth   32
Measuring earthquakes   34

Do-it-yourself seismograph 36
Slips and faults   38
Building fold mountains   40
Fire down below   42
Moving magma   44
Erupting volcanoes   46
Volcanic shapes   48
Vicious gases   50
Steaming hot   52
Volcanic rocks   54
Making crystals   56
Glass and bubbles   58
Layers on layers   60

What's a fossil?   62
Hard as nails!   64
Testing for minerals   66

Natural Wonders Close to Home

What is soil?   70
Examining soil   72
Tree study   74
Looking at bark   76
Specimen collection   78
How plants grow   80
Reaching for light   82
Natural water pumps   84
Seeds and plant life   86
Growing from fruit   88
Life in the forest   90
Soil erosion   92
The balance of life   94
Animal tracks
and footprints   96

Searching for insects   98
What is an insect?   100
Studying insect life   102
Insects in disguise   104
Insects to watch   106
Moths and butterflies   108
Watching a caterpillar grow 110
Crawling colonies   112
Discovering birds   114
Bird-watching   116
Listening to birds   118
Bird's nests   120
Feed the birds   122
Tell-tale bird traces   124
Bird travel and flight   126

Physical and Material Marvels

Chemical change 130
Tests with yeast 132
Preservation and decay 134
Stone and concrete 136
Building bridges 138
Tunnel construction 140
The strength of a pyramid 142
Surveying a site 144
Powerful levers 146
Levers at work 148
The power of energy 150
Wind and water power 152
Energy from liquid and air 154

How magnets work 156
Magnetic Earth 158
Magnets and maps 160
Electric magnets 162
Computer data storage 164
Fun with magnets 166
Magnet sports 168
Images from light 170
Cameras and light 172
A photographic image
  on film 174
Getting in focus 176
Letting in the light 178

How telescopes work 180
Satellites and orbits 182
Power boost in Space 184
Listen to this 186

Travel and Transport

Simple boats 190
Sail power 192
How ships float 194
What's in a hull? 196
Ship stability 198
Power and steering afloat 200
Safety measures at sea 202
Submarine action 204
Making rails 206
Rolling stock 208
Locomotive 210
Brake van 212
Monorail 214
Making car wheels turn 216
Changing gear 218
Car control 220
Keeping cool 222

Prototype car 224
Parachutes and balloons 226
Streamlined design 228
Curve and lift 230
Jet propulsion 232
Propeller flight 234
Model planes 236

Escaping from Earth 238
Rocket launch 240
Going to the Moon 242
Artificial gravity 244
Working in Space 246

Glossary 248   Index 252   Acknowledgements 256

Science at Home

S cience is the search for truth and knowledge. It is the process of finding information about the world around us. It tries to answer questions about how it works. Scientists are people who gather this knowledge of the world. They develop techniques for investigating how things work. They work in controlled environments, such as laboratories, so that they can study results. We call this experimentation.

Why experiment?

Experiments help you discover and understand how things work and why things happen. When you try ideas out, concepts that seem hard to grasp become easier to understand. This is why scientists experiment – to test their ideas. By experimenting, people invent and perfect machines and processes that make our lives easier. Today, the quality of our lives depends on science for everyday comfort, health and entertainment, transport and communication.

Innovation and change

This book of experiments demonstrates many of the breakthroughs and discoveries that have had an impact on our lives. The technique of asking questions and trying to answer them through observation and experiment is important to science. The continuous process of discovery and experiment means that scientists come up with different answers. This is why science is always changing. Innovations and inventions change the way we look at the world, so we see it differently. Imagine, for example, what people must have thought the stars were before the telescope was invented to help them see the heavens more clearly.

Finding your way around this book

This book is divided into four sections of experiments. Each section explores various specialized areas of science within an everyday theme:

Our Restless Earth looks at the Earth's formation. You will see how weather and geological activities, such as volcanoes and earthquakes, affect the shape of the land.

Natural Wonders Close to Home explores nature and the environment by discovering the habitats in your own garden or in nearby woods and parks.

Physical and Material Marvels investigates the basic principles of physics and chemistry, from how machines work to construction and building. This section focuses on power and energy, chemical change, light and cameras, electricity and magnets.

Finally, *Travel and Transport* explores how trains, cars, airplanes, rockets and ships have developed through history to the present day. This section will also explain how each of these machines work.

EXPERIMENTING HINTS

• Before you start, tell an adult what you are going to do. Show him or her the experiment and explain where and how you intend to do it.
• Make sure you have all the necessary items required for the project and that the materials and equipment are clean. You should be able to find everything you need either in your home or from a local store.
• Read the whole project first. Then read each step and make sure you understand it before you begin. All the experiments in this book are safe as long as you follow the instructions exactly, and ask for adult help when advised to do so.
• When you have finished a project, clear everything away safely, especially breakable items, such as glass. Remember to wash your hands!
• Take extra care with experiments that involve electricity, heating things up, handling chemicals, soil and glass. If you are using any food, make sure you have permission to use it and throw it away after you have finished. If a project advises using gloves, be sure to do so.
• Do not worry if an experiment doesn't work or you miss what happens. Try to work out why it has gone wrong and do the experiment again. It's all part of the fun!

Our Restless Earth

Earthquakes and volcanoes are a reminder that the Earth's surface is constantly and dramatically changing. Fossils reveal how many kinds of plants and animals that were once alive have now disappeared. Scientists realize that it is part of the Earth's nature to undergo violent changes caused by natural processes that act over billions of years. In the following pages, you can discover how some of these natural processes, such as wind erosion, rivers and mountain formation, affect the Earth.

Spinning planet

North Pole

beams of sunlight

Equator

South Pole

The Earth is like a giant ball spinning in Space. The only light falling on it is the light of the Sun, glowing 150 million km/ 93 million miles away. The Earth turns once a day, and it orbits the Sun once a year. The experiments on these pages investigate the two ways of moving, and explain why night and day, and the seasons, occur. The ball represents the Earth and the torch (flashlight), the Sun. In the final project, you can make a thermometer using water to record changes in temperature from night to day, and from season to season.

▲ Variable sunlight

The Sun's light does not fall evenly over the Earth, because our planet is round. Imagine three identical beams of sunlight falling on the Earth. One falls on the Equator, and the others on the North and South Poles. The beam falling on the Equator covers a much smaller area, so its energy is more concentrated and the temperature is higher.

YOU WILL NEED

Night and day: felt-tipped pen, plastic ball, thin string, non-hardening modelling material, torch (flashlight).

The seasons: felt-tipped pen, plastic ball, bowl just big enough for the ball to sit on, torch (flashlight), books or a box to set the torch on.

Make a thermometer: water, bottle, food dye, clear straw, reusable adhesive, thin card, scissors, felt-tipped pen.

Night and day

I Draw or stick a shape on the ball to represent your country. Stick the string to the ball with modelling material. Tie the string to a rail, such as a towel rail, so that the ball hangs freely.

2 Shine the torch on the ball. If the country you live in is on the half of the ball in shadow on the far side, then it is night, because it is facing away from the Sun.

3 Your home country may be on the half of the ball lit by the torch instead. If so, it must be daytime here because it is facing the Sun. Keep the torch level, aimed at the middle.

4 Turn the ball from left to right. As you turn the ball, your country will move from the light half to the dark half. You can see how the Sun comes up and goes down as the Earth turns.

The seasons

1 Use the felt-tipped pen to draw a line around the middle of the ball. This represents the Equator. Sit the ball on top of the bowl, so that the Equator line is sloping gently.

2 Put the torch on the books so that it shines just above the Equator. It is summer on the half of the ball above the Equator where the torch is shining, and winter on the other half of the world.

3 Shine the torch on the Equator. It sheds equal light in each half of the ball. This is the equivalent of spring and autumn, when days and nights are a similar length throughout the world.

Solar power ▶

The Sun pours energy on to the Earth as heat and light. The amount of energy received in any one place on the Earth changes with the seasons. This is because the Earth's axis is tilted. In the summer, one half of the Earth tilts toward the Sun, and is warmer. In the winter, it tilts away from the Sun and is colder.

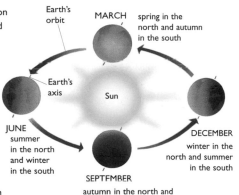

Earth's orbit

Earth's axis

Sun

MARCH spring in the north and autumn in the south

JUNE summer in the north and winter in the south

DECEMBER winter in the north and summer in the south

SEPTEMBER autumn in the north and spring in the south

Make a thermometer

1 Pour cold water into the bottle until it is about two-thirds full. Add some food dye. Dip the straw into the water, and seal the neck tightly with reusable adhesive.

4 On a hot day, the Sun's heat will make the air and water expand, forcing the water level in the straw above the room temperature mark. Cool the thermometer in the refrigerator. Mark the different levels with a pen.

2 Blow down the straw to force some extra air into the bottle. After a few seconds, the extra air pressure inside will force the water level to rise up the straw.

3 Cut the card and slot it in over the straw. Let the bottle stand for a while. Make a mark on the card by the water level to show room temperature. Take your thermometer outside.

Phases of the Moon

The Moon is the closest celestial entity to Earth. We know more about the Moon than about any other heavenly body because astronauts explored its surface. The Moon is Earth's only satellite. It measures 3,476 km/2,160 miles across, about a quarter of the size of the Earth. It circles the Earth at a distance of about 385,000km/239,000 miles, and makes the journey about once a month. The Moon does not give out any light of its own. We see it because it reflects light from the Sun. The sunlight illuminates different parts of the Moon as the month goes by. This makes the Moon seem to change shape. The Moon spins around slowly as it circles the Earth, so the same side is always turned toward the Earth.

We only see the Moon lit up completely once a month, but you do not have to wait a month to see the changes in its shape or phases. The project here will show you in just a few minutes how the Moon goes through its phases!

▲ **Face of the Moon**
This picture shows a view of the Moon from the Earth. When the whole of the Moon is lit up like this, we call it a full Moon. The darker regions on the surface are great, dusty plains called seas, or maria. The lighter areas are highlands. These are pitted with craters that can be hundreds of kilometres/ miles across. Mountains on the Moon rise to more than 6,000m/18,000ft.

Make your own Moon

YOU WILL NEED
inflatable ball, glue, glue brush, glass, foil, scissors, reusable adhesive, torch (flashlight).

1 Make sure that you have washed and dried your ball thoroughly before using! Paint glue all over the ball. Rest it on a glass or something similar, to keep it still.

2 Carefully cut the tinfoil into large square sheets. Wrap up the ball in the foil. Try to make sure that the wrapping is as smooth as possible. You now have your Moon!

3 Place your Moon on a table. Wedge a small ball of reusable adhesive under the ball. This will hold it firm and stop it from rolling off the table.

4 Get your friend to stand at one side of the table to shine a torch with a strong beam on your Moon. Go to the opposite side of the table. Look at your Moon with the main lights out.

5 Gradually move around the table, still looking at your Moon, which is lit up one side by the torch. You will see the different shapes it takes. These shapes are the Moon's phases.

Going through the phases ▶

When you are opposite your friend in the project, the side of the ball facing you is dark. This is what happens once a month in the night sky. We can only see a thin sliver of light, which we call a new or crescent Moon. As you move around the table, more of the ball is lit by the torch. All of it will be lit when you are behind your friend. When this happens to the real Moon, we describe it as full. As you continue moving around, the ball gradually fades into darkness. When you are opposite your friend again, you will see a new Moon again.

crescent Moon

first quarter phase

full Moon

last quarter phase

crescent Moon

The rise and fall of tides

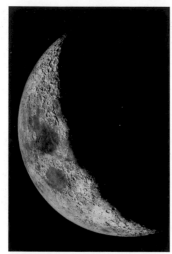

▲ **The lunar cycle**
The Moon is a lifeless desert of rock. It has no atmosphere to protect it from the Sun's dangerous rays, and no water to sustain life. The shape of the Moon appears to change during the month. We call these changes in shape the Moon's phases. It takes the Moon 29½ days to change from a slim crescent to a full circle and back again.

The Earth appears blue from the darkness of Space. This is because more than 70 percent of its surface is covered with oceans. The seas make up more than one million million million tons of seawater.

Every 12 hours or so, the seawater rises, then falls back again. These rises and falls are called the tides. When the water is rising, we say the tide is flowing. When it is falling, we say the tide is ebbing. The movement of the ocean waters is caused by the Moon and by the Earth spinning. Gravity pulls the Moon and Earth together. As the Earth turns, the Moon pulls at the ocean water directly beneath it, causing the water to rise. A similar rise in sea level occurs on the opposite side of the Earth, where the water bulges out as a result of the Earth spinning. At these places, there is a high tide. Some six hours later, the Earth has turned 90°. The sea then falls to its lowest point and there is a low tide.

The two experiments opposite explain how the oceans rise and fall without any change in the amount of seawater, and how the tidal bulges of water stay in the same place below the Moon, as the Earth spins beneath it.

How tides occur

Tides rise beneath the Moon as the Earth turns. The gravity of the Moon tugs at the oceans, pulling the water around with it.

Once every two weeks, the Sun and the Moon line up with the Earth. Their combined pull creates a spring tide, where the tides are higher than usual.

One week later, the Sun and the Moon are at right angles to each other. Pulling in different directions, they create a lower tide than usual, called a neap tide.

High and low tide

1 Place the bowl on a firm, flat surface, then half fill it with water. Place the ball gently in the water so that it floats in the middle of the bowl, as shown in the picture.

2 Place both hands on top of the ball, and push it gently but firmly down into the water. Look what happens to the level of the water. It rises in a "high tide".

3 Let the ball gently rise again. Now you can see the water in the bowl dropping again. So the tide has risen and fallen, even though the amount of water is unchanged.

The tidal bulge

YOU WILL NEED

High and low tide: plastic bowl, water, plastic ball to represent the world.

The tidal bulge: strong glue, one 20cm/8in length and two 40cm/16in lengths of thin string, plastic ball to represent the world, plastic bowl, hand drill, water.

1 Glue the 20cm/8in length of the string very firmly to the ball and leave it to dry. Meanwhile, ask an adult to drill two holes in the rim of the bowl, one on each side.

2 Thread a 40cm/16in length of string through each hole, and knot the string around the rim. Half fill the plastic bowl with water and float the ball in the water.

3 Ask a friend to pull the string on the ball toward him or her. There is now more water on one side of the ball than the other. This is called a tidal bulge.

4 The Moon pulls on the water as well as the Earth. So now ask the friend to hold the ball in place, while both of you pull out the strings attached to the bowl until it distorts.

5 There is now a tidal bulge on each side of the world. One of you slowly turn the ball. Now you can see how, in effect, the tidal bulges move around the world as the world turns.

Ocean waves and currents

▲ Powerful seas

In stormy weather, giant waves rear up and crash down, turning the sea into a raging turmoil.

The sea is rarely still. Even on a calm day, you will see ripples on the surface. Waves move over the ocean's surface. They are driven mainly by the wind. The stronger the winds, and the longer the fetch (the distance they have traveled), the bigger and higher the waves are. Waves usually only affect the surface of the water. As they travel, the water itself does not move. It just moves up and down as the wave passes through it. At a very deep level in some oceans, the water does move in giant streams called ocean currents. These can be hot or cold, and can affect the world's climate. Ocean currents are usually caused by differences in the water's saltiness or temperature, rather than by the wind.

The first project shows how waves are made, and the second, how currents are set up by the wind blowing. Currents such as the ones in the third project happen on a much larger scale in the world's major oceans.

wave approaches float

float maintains position

wave travels, float does not

▲ Wave goodbye

The diagrams above show how waves travel across the water surface, while objects floating on the water hardly move at all.

Making waves

YOU WILL NEED
rectangular plastic bowl, jug (pitcher), water, bathtub or inflatable pool, non-hardening modelling material.

1 Place the bowl on the floor or on a table. Choose a place where it does not matter if a little water spills over. Fill the bowl with water until it almost reaches the brim.

2 Blow very gently over the surface of the water. You will see that the water begins to ripple where you blow on it. This is how ocean waves are formed by air movement.

3 Fill the bathtub or pool with water. Blow gently along the length of the bath or pool. Blow at the same strength as in step 2, and from the same height above the water.

4 Keep blowing for a minute or so. Notice that the waves are bigger in the bathtub or pool, even though you are not blowing harder. This is because they reach farther across the water.

5 Now drop a small piece of modelling material into the water. Watch how it sets up waves. Ripples travel out in circles from where the modelling material entered the water.

Ocean currents

YOU WILL NEED

rectangular plastic bowl, jug (pitcher), water, talcum powder.

1 Place the bowl on the floor or on a table. Choose a place where it does not matter if a little water spills over. Fill the bowl with water until it almost reaches the rim.

2 Scatter a small amount of talcum powder over the water. Use just enough powder to make a very fine film over the water's surface. The less you use, the better.

3 Blow very gently across the water from the middle of one side of the bowl to the other. You will see how the water starts to move. Ocean currents begin to move in the same way.

4 Keep blowing, and the powder swirls in two circles as it hits the far side. This is what happens when currents hit continents. One current turns clockwise, the other turns anticlockwise.

Changing coastlines

Of all the natural forces that erode (wear away) the land, the sea is the most powerful. It carries sand particles that act like a grindstone on the shore. Waves are forced into cracks in the rocks. They widen the cracks, eventually breaking up the rock face. Huge cliffs are carved out of mountains, broad platforms are sliced back through rocks, and houses are left dangling over the edges of the land.

river estuary

mudflats and lagoons

spit

groynes

bayhead beach

stump

sea stack

headland

sea arch

New land can also be created at the ocean's edge. Where headland cliffs are being eroded by waves, the bays between may fill with sand. On coasts where the sea is shallow, waves build beaches of shingle, sand, and mud. The first experiment demonstrates the destructive effect of the sea when it hits the shore. The second project shows how waves make ripples on sandy beaches.

▲ Everchanging landscape

The sea's power to build and destroy a coastline can be seen in this picture. Coastal areas that are exposed to the full force of the waves are eroded into steep cliffs. Headlands are worn back, leaving behind stacks, stumps, and arches. In more sheltered places, the sand piles up to form beaches, or waves may carry material along the coast to build spits and mudflats.

▲ Relentless assault

The sea is at its most spectacular at the edges of big oceans, where the waves are big and powerful. In time, their continuous assault on the land will break up the toughest rocks into tiny pieces.

Attacking the shore

1 Mix a little water with the sand in a bucket, until it is very wet and sticks firmly together. Then pack the sand into a wedge shape at one end of the tank.

2 Carefully pour water into the empty end of the tank, so as not to disturb the sand too much. Fill the tank until the water level comes about two-thirds of the way up the sloping sand.

3 Make gentle waves in the water on the opposite side of the sand. Notice how the waves gradually wear away the sloping sand. This is what happens on a sandy seashore.

How ripples are formed in sand

YOU WILL NEED

Making waves: sand, plastic bucket, water tank, water, jug (pitcher).

How ripples are formed in sand: heavy filled round can, round dishwashing bowl, jug (pitcher), water, fine, clean sand, spoon.

---

1 Place a heavy can in the middle of the dishwashing bowl, then fill the bowl with water to at least half way. The water should not cover more than two-thirds of the can.

2 Sprinkle a little sand into the bowl to create a thin layer about 5mm/¼in deep. Spread the sand until it is even, then let it settle into a flat layer at the bottom of the bowl.

3 Stir the water gently with the spoon. Drag the spoon in a circle around the can. As the water begins to swirl, stir faster with the spoon, but keep the movement smooth.

4 As you stir faster, lift the spoon out and let the water swirl around by itself. The sand will start to develop ripples. As you stir faster, the ripples become more defined.

Water on the move

Rivers start high in the hills and wind their way down toward the sea, or sometimes, a lake. At its start, a river is a tiny stream tumbling down the slopes. It is formed by rain running off a mountainside, or by water bubbling up from a spring. As the water flows downhill, it is joined by other streams and grows bigger.

The first project shows how water shapes the landscape by physically eroding (wearing away) the rock. The second experiment demonstrates how in some places, erosion can be a chemical process, in which water dissolves the rock and carries it away.

Over millions of years, a river can carve a gorge deep through solid rock, or deposit (lay down) a vast plain of fine mud called silt. The great rivers of the world take millions of tons of mud, rock, and sand from the land every day and carry them into the sea. If the river meets a low-lying shoreline, the sediment is dropped. It may spread out into a fan-shaped muddy plain called a delta. When this happens, the river is forced to branch out into smaller streams as it flows into the sea. You can see how this happens in the third experiment.

upper reaches

middle reaches

lower reaches

◀ The course of a river
As it moves across the land, a river changes in character. In the upper reaches, it is a fast-flowing, tumbling stream that cuts down through steep, narrow valleys. Lower down, it broadens and deepens into a river. Eventually, it moves across a broad floodplain before reaching the sea.

The destructive power of water

1 Put one end of a baking sheet on a brick. Put the other end of the baking sheet on a lower tray or bowl, so that it slopes downward. Make a sandcastle on the baking sheet.

2 Slowly drip water over the sandcastle. Watch the sand crumble and form a new shape. This happens because the sand erodes away where the water hits it.

3 Make sure that the water flows down the middle of the baking sheet. This way, the water hits the middle of the sand castle, eroding the middle to form a natural stack.

Chemical erosion

1 Build a pile of brown sugar on a baking sheet. Imagine it is a mountain made of a soluble rock (that dissolves in water). Press the sugar down firmly, and shape it to a point.

2 Drip water on your sugar mountain. It will erode as the water dissolves the sugar. The water running off should be brown, because it contains dissolved brown sugar.

Making a delta

1 Use scissors to trim the top of the cardboard container so that it is about 10–15cm/4–6in deep. Now take the two plastic garbage bags to make the box waterproof.

2 Cover the inside of the box with the garbage bags and tape them securely at each end of the box. Make sure that the seal between the garbage bags is secure.

3 Using the trowel, carefully spread a layer of sand over the bottom of the sheet until the sand is about 4–5cm/1½-2in deep. Flatten the sand with the trowel until it is smooth.

4 Rest one end of the container on a woodblock or something similar, to make a slope. Pour water from the jug on to the sand in the middle of the higher end.

5 If you continue pouring, you will find that the water gradually washes away a gully through the sand. It deposits sand it has washed away at the lower end in a delta region.

Cloud and rain

Water moves around the Earth and its atmosphere in a continuous process called the water cycle. Heat from the Sun causes water from oceans, lakes, and rivers to evaporate into water vapour. Water is also released into the atmosphere from plants in a process called transpiration. Flowers and trees take up water from their roots. They use some and release the rest back out through their leaves – water vapour rises into the atmosphere. It cools as it rises, and changes back into tiny droplets of liquid water. This is called condensation. The droplets gather together and form clouds. When the water in the atmosphere becomes too heavy to be held in the air, it returns to the Earth's surface as precipitation (dew, rain, sleet and snow). The land has a fresh supply of water, and so the water cycle continues.

The first experiment shows you how water changes to vapour and back again, when a cold surface makes the water vapour condense into water droplets. In the second project, you can make a simple rain gauge to measure the amount of rain you get where you live. If you live in a desert region, you may have to wait a long time!

cloud of ice crystals

cloud of water droplets

water vapour rises

▲ Forming clouds

Clouds form when warm air containing water vapour rises into the air and cools. The vapour turns into droplets of water, forming clouds. If the air is very cold, the vapour turns into a cloud of tiny ice crystals.

YOU WILL NEED
heat-proof jug (pitcher), water, pan, oven gloves, plate.

Water vapour

1 Fill up the jug with water from the hot water tap. Pour the water into the pan. Switch on one of the rings on the stove and place the pan on it.

2 Heat the water until it is boiling and steam is rising. Lift the plate with the oven gloves. Hold it upside down above the pan. After a few minutes, turn off the heat.

3 Take the plate away, using the oven gloves. You will see that the plate is covered with drops of water. This is vapour that has cooled and turned back into liquid.

Measuring rainfall

cirrus

cirrostratus

cirrocumulus

altostratus

altocumulus

cumulonimbus

stratocumulus

cumulus

stratus

▲ Cloud spotter

The main kinds of clouds in the sky can be grouped according to how far they are above the Earth's surface. High clouds include cirrus clouds. Altostratus and altocumulus are middle clouds. Stratus and cumulus clouds are low ones.

1 Cut a strip of masking tape the same height as the jar. Stick it on the outsideof the jar. Use a ruler and pencil to mark 1cm/½in intervals on the masking tape.

2 Place the funnel in the jar. Put the gauge outside in an open space away from trees. Look at the gauge at the same time each day. Has it rained in the last 24 hours?

3 If it has rained, use the scale to see how much water is in the jar. This is the rainfall for the past 24 hours. Make a note of the reading. Empty the jar before you return it to its place.

4 You can measure rainfall more accurately if you use a separate, narrower measuring jar. Stick another strip of masking tape along the side of this jar. Pour water into the large collecting jar up to the 1cm/½in mark. Then pour the water into the narrow jar. Mark 1cm/½in where the water level reaches. Divide the length from the bottom of the jar to the 1cm/½in mark into 10 equal parts. Each will be equivalent to 1mm/¹⁄₁₆in of rainfall. You can now extend the scale past the 1cm/½in mark to the top of the narrow jar. Use this jar to measure the rainfall you collect to the nearest 1mm/¹⁄₁₆in, just as professional meteorologists do.

What is humidity?

The temperature of a place is mainly controlled by the amount of heat it absorbs from the Sun. Another factor is altitude (how high the land is). Areas at very high altitudes are colder than areas at sea level. The distance from the sea also affects temperature. The sea has a moderating effect. You can see how this works in the first project. Water takes more time to heat up than the land, but it holds its heat for much longer. Therefore, summers are cooler and winters milder on the coast than inland.

A temperature of 21°C/70°F in the Caribbean feels much hotter than 21°C/70°F in Egypt. This is due to humidity – the amount of water vapour in the air. When there is high humidity, the air feels moist and sticky. The perspiration on our skin cannot evaporate, since there is too much water in the air already. When there is little water vapour in the air, the air feels dry. The perspiration on our skin escapes more easily and cools us down. The second experiment shows you how to measure humidity using a simple device called a hygrometer. When the air is very humid, there is more of a chance that it will rain.

▲ **Water from plants**

Plants play a vital role in creating humidity. A plant's leaves give off water vapour in a process called transpiration. Cover a plant with a clear plastic bag. Seal the plastic around the pot with adhesive tape. Put the plant in direct sunlight for two hours. Notice that the bag starts to get misty, and droplets of water form on the inside. They form when the water vapour given off by the plant turns back to a liquid.

Measuring temperature changes

YOU WILL NEED

Measuring temperature changes: two bowls, jug (pitcher) of water, sand, watch, thermometer, notebook, pen.
Measuring humidity: one sheet of red and one sheet of green thin card, scissors, ruler, pen, glue, toothpick, used matchstick, straw, reusable adhesive, blotting paper, hole punch.

1 Pour water into one bowl and sand into the other bowl. You do not need to measure the exact quantities of sand and water – just use roughly equal amounts.

2 Place the bowls side by side in a cool place. Leave them for a few hours. Then note the temperature of the sand and water. The temperature of each should be about the same.

3 Place the bowls side by side in the sunlight. Leave the bowls for an hour or two. Then measure and record the temperatures of the sand and water in each bowl.

4 Put each bowl in a cool place indoors. Measure and record the temperature of the sand and water every 15 minutes. The sand cools down faster than the water.

5 In this experiment, the sand acts like land and the water acts like the ocean. The sand gets hot quicker, but the water holds its heat longer. Dip your hands in to feel the difference.

Measuring humidity

1 Cut out a rectangle from green card. Mark regular intervals along one side. Cut a 2cm/¾in slit in one short side. Split the parts and glue them to a red card base.

2 Cut another long rectangle from the green card. Fold it and stick it to the card base as shown above. Pierce the top carefully with a toothpick to make a pivot.

3 Attach the used matchstick to one end of the straw using some reusable adhesive, to make a pointer. Both the matchstick and the adhesive give the pointer some weight.

4 Carefully cut out several squares of blotting paper. Use the hole punch to make a hole in the middle of each square. Slide the squares over the flat end of the pointer.

5 Now carefully pierce the pointer with the toothpick pivot. Position the pointer as shown above. Make sure that the pointer can swing freely up and down.

6 Adjust the position of the toothpick so that it stays level. Take the hygrometer into the bathroom and run a bath. The humidity makes the blotting paper damp. The pointer tips upward.

The way the wind blows

The wind is moving air. Wind can move dust, sand and other small items. The first experiment shows how the weight of a particle affects how far it travels. The wind also causes changes in the weather. Meteorologists study the wind to help them predict these changes. They use a weather vane to find out its direction. The second project shows how to make a simple weather vane. Wind speed is measured using an anemometer. This device consists of a circle of cups that spin when the wind blows, like a windmill. The faster the wind blows, the faster the anemometer spins.

YOU WILL NEED

How wind sorts sand: two empty ice cube trays, piece of thin card large enough to fit over an ice cube tray, spoon, mix of fine and coarse sand, hairdryer.

Make a weather vane: reusable adhesive, plastic pot and its lid, scissors, garden stick, two plastic straws, thin blue card, pen, adhesive tape, pin, plywood, compass.

parabolic dune

transverse dune

wind direction

barchan dune

seif dune

◄ Name that dune

Some deserts contain vast seas of sand, called ergs, where the wind piles sand up into dunes. The shape of the dune depends on the amount of sand and changeability of the wind direction. Crescent-shaped dunes, called parabolic dunes, are common on the coasts. The ones with narrow points facing away from the wind are called barchans. These dunes creep slowly forwards. Transverse dunes form at right angles to the main wind direction. Seifs occur where there is little sand, and wind comes from different directions.

How wind sorts sand

1 Turn one ice cube tray over, and lay it down end to end with another ice cube tray. Place the card over the upturned tray, and spoon the sand over it to make a sand dune.

2 Hold a hairdryer close to the upturned tray, pointing it towards the other tray. Turn the hairdryer on, so that it blows sand into the open ice cube tray.

3 Look at the grains in each box. The distance a grain travels depends on its weight. Heavy grains fall in the end of the tray nearest to you. Light grains are blown to the farthest end.

Make a weather vane

1 Stick a ball of reusable adhesive to the middle of the lid of the pot. Ask an adult to pierce a hole in the bottom of the pot with the scissors. Place the pot on top of the lid.

2 Slide the stick into one of the straws. Trim the end of the stick so that it is a little shorter than the straw. Push the straw and stick through the hole in the pot and into the adhesive.

3 Cut out a square of card. Mark each corner with a point of the compass – N, E, S, W. Fold in half and snip a hole in the middle. Carefully slip the card over the straw.

4 Cut out two card triangles. Stick them to each end of the second straw to form an arrow head and tail. Put a ball of reusable adhesive in the top of the first straw in the pot.

5 Push a pin through the middle of the arrow. Stick the pin into the reusable adhesive in the first straw. Be careful not to prick your finger when you handle the pin.

6 Attach your weather vane to a plywood base using a piece of reusable adhesive. Test it for use – the arrow should spin around freely when you blow on it.

7 Take your weather vane outside and use a compass to point it in the right direction. You can now discover the direction the wind is blowing.

Turning the sails ▶

The miniature windmills on this toy spin faster the harder you blow on them. The sails of real windmills also spin faster as the speed of the wind increases. As a result, windmills need a 'governor'. This device regulates the speed of the sails' rotation, so they are not damaged in very windy weather.

Recording weather

Meteorologists gather information about the weather from satellites, balloons, and other instruments. Powerful computers help them to analyze the data. Using this information, meteorologists draw weather maps. These can show the state of the weather at any one time, or they can be a forecast of weather in the future. The maps use symbols to represent conditions such as rainfall and wind direction.

You can set up your own weather station to record daily conditions with a few simple devices. You will be able to use some of the instruments you have made in other projects, such as the weather vane, hygrometer and rain gauge. You will also need to buy a thermometer to measure the temperature. Take measurements with your weather instruments every day. Write them down in a special weather book. Also, make a note of what the weather is like in general – fine, cloudy, drizzly, frosty and so on. Don't forget to make a note of the date!

Meteorologists look at records from the past to discover changes in climate. The project opposite shows you how to make your own discoveries about climate changes, by looking at the record of tree growth.

▲ Forecasting rain
A hygrometer will gauge the amount of moisture in the air. When the pointer tilts up on the scale, the air is moist and rain may be on the way.

▲ Measuring rainfall
A rain gauge will tell you how much rain has fallen. Rainfall is collected over a set period in a jar or measuring bottle, and the amount is recorded.

▲ Wind direction
A windmill shows how hard the wind is blowing. A weather vane will tell you the wind's direction. The arrow points in the direction that the wind is blowing from. So if the arrow points west, the wind is a west wind.

The wooden weather record

1 Ask a tree surgeon, the local council or a sawmill for a newly cut slice of log. Use the paintbrush to brush away the dust and dirt from the slice of wood.

2 When the log slice is clean, examine it closely. Look at the pattern of rings. They are small in the middle, and get bigger and bigger toward the outer edge of the log.

3 Each ring is a year's growth. So count the rings out from the middle carefully. This tells you how old the tree is. If there are 105 rings, for instance, the tree is 105 years old.

4 Using a ruler, measure the width of each ring. Start from the middle and work outward. Ask a friend to write down the widths as you call them out.

width of ring (in mm/¹⁄₁₆in)

5 On graph paper, mark five squares for each year along the bottom. Mark widths for the rings up the side, five squares for each 1mm/¹⁄₁₆in. Plot your measurements as dots for each year.

6 Join the dots with a line. This line shows how the weather has changed with each year. If the line is going up, the weather was warmer so the tree grew a lot. If the line falls, the weather was colder so the tree grew less.

Broken Earth

The surface of the Earth is not one piece but cracked, like a broken eggshell, into giant slabs. There are about 20 of these huge pieces of rock which are called tectonic plates. Tectonic plates are not held in one place, but slide around the Earth. They move very slowly – at about the pace of a fingernail growing. But tectonic plates are so gigantic that their movement has dramatic effects on the Earth's surface. Earthquakes and volcanoes happen where plates slide apart or past each other, or collide. Colliding plates also push up mountain ranges.

The continents drift around the world on tectonic plates. Once, they were all joined together in one huge continent called Pangaea. Around 200 million years ago, the tectonic plates beneath Pangaea began to move apart, carrying fragments of the continent with them. These fragments slowly drifted into the positions they are in now. The experiment opposite demonstrates how the continents may have once been, and how they move.

▲ **Patterns of earthquakes**
The Earth's rigid shell is called the lithosphere, from the Greek word lithos (stone). It is broken into the huge fragments shown on this map. The African plate is gigantic, underlying not only Africa, but half of the Atlantic Ocean too. The Cocos plate under the West Indies is much smaller. Black dots mark the origins of major earthquakes over a year. See how they coincide with the plate margins.

ocean   plates pulling apart   mid-ocean ridge

mantle   rising magma   plate

▲ **Pulling apart**
Right down the middle of the sea bed in the Atlantic Ocean, there is a giant crack where the tectonic plates are pulling apart. Molten (melted) rock from the Earth's interior wells up into the crack. As it cools, it solidifies (becomes solid) to form the mid-ocean ridge.

continental crust wrinkles up   continental plate

ocean trench

ocean

ocean plate

ocean plate descends

▲ **Pushing together**
In many places, tectonic plates slowly crunch together with enormous force. As they collide, one plate may be forced under the other. Earthquakes and volcanoes are often the result.

A continental jigsaw

atlas, pencil, sheets of tracing paper, tape, sheets of green, purple and red thin card, scissors, paper clips, two boxes.

1 Find the continents of North and South America, Europe, and Africa in an atlas. Trace the outlines of the shape of these continents on to tracing paper.

2 Stick the tracing paper on to green, purple and red sheets of card. Then carefully cut around the outlines of the continents you have drawn from the atlas.

3 Move the eastern (right-hand) coasts of North and South America up to the western (left-hand) coasts of Europe and Africa to see how well they fit together.

4 You will find that the coastlines of the Americas, Europe, and Africa fit together very well. Scientists believe that these continents were once joined together in this way.

5 The continents of the Americas, Europe, and Africa sit on plates that are moving in opposite directions. Use the continent cards you have made in the above project to see how they drift apart. Fold a large sheet of card in half, and attach paper clips along the fold. Drape it over two boxes. Stick the Americas on one sheet, and Europe and Africa on the other. Push upward on the fold, and see the continents move apart.

Restless Earth

The movement of rocks that causes earthquakes usually occurs deep inside the Earth's crust. The exact point at which the rocks start to break is known as the focus. This can lie as deep as hundreds of km/miles or as close as tens of km/miles down. The most violent disturbance on the surface occurs at a point directly above the focus, called the

YOU WILL NEED

Tremors: set of dominoes, card.

Quakes: scissors, strong rubber band, ruler, plastic seed tray (without holes), piece of thin card, salt.

epicentre. The closer the focus is, the more destructive the earthquake. San Francisco, in California, sits near a line of weakness in the Earth's crust known as the San Andreas Fault. The fault marks the boundary of the eastern Pacific plate and the North American plate. As they try to slide past each other, they make the ground shake violently. Earthquakes and volcanoes occur around the boundaries of all the plates on the Earth's surface.

▲ Earthquake alert

Most earthquakes originate many kilometres/miles below the surface, at the focus. The most intense vibrations on the surface are felt immediately above the focus, at the epicentre.

Tremors

1 This project investigates how energy in earthquake waves (tremors) varies with distance. Near the end of a table, build a simple house out of dominoes. Stand them up on their edges.

2 Place the cardboard on the dominoes to make the roof of your house. Many people in earthquake zones live in the simplest of houses, built not too differently from this one.

3 Go to the opposite end of the table and hit it with your hand, but not too hard. Your domino house probably shakes, but still stays standing. Now hit the table at the other end.

4 The waves you create when you hit the table are strong enough to knock down the house. When you hit the other end of the table, the waves are too weak to knock it down.

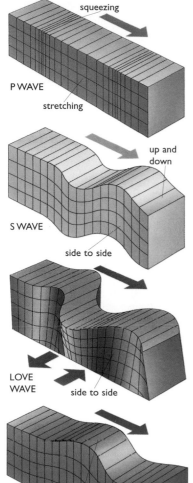

P WAVE — squeezing — stretching

S WAVE — up and down — side to side

LOVE WAVE — side to side

RAYLEIGH WAVE — rippling up and down

▲ How earthquakes move

The enormous energy released by an earthquake travels through the ground in the form of waves. The P (primary) wave compresses, then stretches rocks it passes through. The S (secondary) wave produces a side-to-side and up-and-down action. Love waves travel on the surface, making the ground move from side to side. Rayleigh waves are surface waves that move up and down.

Quakes

1 With the scissors, cut the rubber band at one end to make a long strip. This represents a layer of rock inside the Earth before it is affected by an earthquake.

2 Measure the rubber strip with a ruler. This represents the original length of the rock in the ground. Make a note of how long the rubber is at this stage.

3 Stretch the rubber band and hold it tightly above the tray. In the same way, rocks get stretched by pulling forces inside the Earth during an earthquake.

4 Ask a friend to hold the card on top of the rubber strip and sprinkle some salt on it. The salt on the card represents the surface of the ground above the stretched rock layer.

5 Now let go of the ends of the rubber strip. Notice how the salt grains on the card are thrown around. This was caused by the energy released when the rubber shrank.

6 Finally, measure the rubber strip again. You will find that it is slightly longer than it was at the start. Rocks are often permanently stretched a little after an earthquake.

Measuring earthquakes

Scientists who study earthquakes are called seismologists. They have a variety of instruments to gather data. The Newton's cradle experiment below explains how waves (tremors) work. The other projects show two ways in which seismologists detect how the ground moves at the beginning of an earthquake. A gravimeter measures small changes in gravity. The tiltmeter detects whether rock layers are tilting.

YOU WILL NEED

Newton's cradle: large beads, wool, adhesive tape, cane, wooden blocks.

Gravimeter: masking tape, ruler, pen, large jar, non-hardening modelling material, rubber band, toothpick, pencil.

Newton's cradle

1 Tie the beads to the ends of the wool threads. Tape the other ends to the cane. Make sure the threads are all the same length, and that the beads just touch when they hang down.

2 Prop up the cane at both ends on a pair of woodblocks supported by more blocks underneath. Secure the ends of the cane with tape. Lift up the bead at one end of the row and let go.

3 The bead at the other end flies up. The energy of the falling bead at one end travels as a pressure wave through the middle ones. It reaches the bead at the other end and pushes it away.

Gravimeter

1 Draw a scale on a strip of masking tape using a ruler and pen. Stick the scale on the jar. On a real instrument, this would measure slight changes in gravity.

2 Bury one end of a rubber band in a ball of modelling material. Stick a toothpick in at right angles to the band, to act as a pointer. Pass the pencil through the loop of the band.

3 Lower the ball into the jar, so that the pointer tip is close to the scale. Attach the pencil on top with modelling material. Move the jar up or down, and the pointer moves down or up the scale.

Tiltmeter

1 Use the hole punch to make a hole in the side of each plastic cup, just about halfway down. Be careful not to prick your fingers. Ask an adult to help you if you prefer.

2 Push one end of the tubing into the hole in one of the cups. Seal it tight with modelling material. Put the other end in the hole in the other cup, and seal it as well.

3 Using the pen, draw identical scales on two strips of the masking tape. Use a ruler and mark regular spaces. Stick the scales at the same height on the side of the cups.

4 Stick the cups to the wooden baseboard with adhesive. Arrange them so that the tube between is pulled straight, but make sure it doesn't pull out.

6 Your tiltmeter is now ready for use. When it is level, the water levels in the cups are the same. When it tilts, the water levels change as water runs through the tube from one cup to the other. Scientists use tiltometers to detect whether rock layers are moving by comparing the water levels in two connected containers.

5 Add food dye to water in the jug, and pour it into each of the cups. Make sure to fill the cups, so that the water level reaches over the openings to the tubes.

Do-it-yourself seismograph

There are hundreds of seismic (from the Greek word *seismos*, meaning earthquake) laboratories around the world. Within minutes of a quake, scientists begin analyzing data from their seismographs. They then compare notes with scientists in other countries.

The Italian scientist, Luigi Palmieri, built the first seismograph in 1856. All seismographs work on the same principle. They have a light frame attached to the ground, and a heavy weight attached to the frame by a spring. The heavy weight has a high inertia, which means it is more difficult to set in motion than a light object. When an earthquake happens, the frame shakes with the ground, but the heavy weight stays in the same place because of inertia. The movement of the frame around the steady weight is recorded by a pen on a roll of paper, which draws a wavy line. The same principle of the inertia of a heavy weight is used to detect tremors in the seismograph shown here.

▲ **Catching the tremors**

The Chinese invented a type of seismograph in AD132. When there was an earthquake, a ball was released from one of the dragons and fell into a frog's mouth. This showed the direction of the vibrations. The instrument detected a earth tremor 500km/300 miles away.

Building a seismograph

YOU WILL NEED
cardboard box, bradawl, tape,
non-hardening modelling material,
pencil, felt-tipped pen, string,
piece of thin card.

1 The cardboard box will become the frame of your seismograph. It needs to be made of very stiff cardboard. The open part of the box will be the front of your instrument.

2 Make a hole in what will be the top of the frame with the bradawl. If the box feels flimsy, strengthen it by taping around the corners, as shown in the picture.

3 Roll a piece of modelling material into a ball, and make a hole in it with the pencil. Push the felt-tipped pen through the modelling material to reach a little way beyond the hole.

4 This will be the pointer of your seismograph and make a record of earthquake vibrations. Tie one end of the piece of string to the top of the pen.

5 Thread the other end of the string through the hole in the top of the box. Now stand the box upright and pull the string through until the pen hangs free.

6 Tie the top end of the string to the pencil, and roll the pencil to take up the slack. When the pen is at the right height (just touching the bottom), tape the pencil into place.

7 Place the card in the bottom of the box underneath the pen. If you have adjusted it properly, the tip of the pen should just touch the card to mark it.

8 Your seismograph is now ready to use. It uses the same principle as a proper seismograph. The heavy bob, or pendulum, will be less affected by shaking motions than the frame.

9 You do not have to wait for an earthquake to test your seismograph. Just shake or tilt the frame. The suspended pen does not move, but it marks the piece of card, giving you your very own seismograph.

Slips and faults

Every earthquake, from the slightest tremor to the violent shaking that destroys buildings, has the same basic cause. Two plates of rock grind past each other along a fault line where the Earth's crust has fractured. Friction between the plates means they do not slide past each other smoothly, but jam and then jump. The first experiment on the opposite page shows how friction at fault lines causes great destructive energy.

Crustal plates float on top of the mantle beneath. The oceanic crust is heavier and denser than the continental crust so it sits lower down. The experiment below demonstrates this.

There are several kinds of fault. When blocks slide past each other horizontally, it is called a transform, or strike-slip fault. In a normal fault, the rocks are pulling apart, and one block slides down the other. In a thrust fault, the blocks are pressing together, causing one to ride up above the other. The second project on the opposite page shows how these movements create landforms, such as mountains and valleys.

direction of movement

fault plane

▲ Making mountains

Fault mountains form by the slow, unstoppable movement of tectonic plates. This puts rocks under such huge stress that they sometimes crack. Such cracks are called faults. Where they occur, huge blocks of rock slip up and down past each other, creating cliffs. In places, a whole series of giant blocks may be thrown up together, creating a new mountain range. The Black Mountains in Germany are an example of block mountains formed in this way.

Floating plates

YOU WILL NEED
woodblock, polystyrene block, bowl of water

1 The two blocks should be about the same size and shape. Polystyrene represents the continental crust, wood the oceanic crust, and water the fluid mantle.

2 Place the blocks in the water. The polystyrene floats higher, because it is less dense, just as the continental crust floats higher on the mantle. Which of the two blocks weighs more?

Fault movements

1 Hold a block in each hand so that the sides of the blocks are touching. Pushing gently, try to make the blocks slide past each other. You will find this easy.

2 Wet the sides of the blocks with the oil, and try to slide them again. You should find that it is easier, because the oil has lessened the friction between the blocks.

3 Pin sheets of sandpaper on the sides of the blocks, and try to make them slide now. You will find it much harder. The sandpaper is rough, and increases friction between the blocks.

Building mountains

YOU WILL NEED

Fault movements: two woodblocks, baby oil, drawing pins (thumb tacks), sheets of sandpaper.

Building mountains: 20cm/8in square sheet of paper, non-hardening modelling material in various shades, rolling pin, modelling tool.

1 On the sheet of paper, roll out several flat sheets of modelling material, each one a different shade. The sheets should be about the same size as the sheet of paper.

2 Place the square, flat sheets of modelling material on top of each other to make a layered block. The different layers are like the layers of rock strata in the Earth's crust.

block mountains

rift valley

3 Lay the layered block flat on the table. With a modelling tool, carefully make two cuts in the clay – one toward the left, and the other toward the right, as shown above.

4 Make two small balls. Lift each of the outside pieces that you have cut on to a ball, as shown above. This forms a block mountain separated by a rift valley.

The crust breaks away at a rift zone where the plates are moving apart. Uplifted rock strata form block mountains, and a descending mass of rock creates the valley.

Building fold mountains

dip

axial plane

strike

Most high mountains are a part of great ranges that stretch for hundreds of kilometres/miles. They may look as though they have been there forever, but geologically they are very young. They have all been thrown up in the last few hundred million years.

The biggest – and youngest – mountain ranges in the world, such as the Himalayas and the Andes, are fold mountains. They started life as flat layers of rock called strata. Layers of rock are laid down over millennia. Some strata form as successive layers of sediments, such as sand, mud and seashells, settle on the ocean floor. Other strata may be made up of molten rock thrown up from the heart of the Earth by volcanoes.

Fold mountains are layers of rock that have been crunched up by pressure – in a similar way to the pressure you will be exerting in these two projects. In real mountain formation, two of the tectonic plates that make up the Earth's surface push against each other, forcing the rock layers along their edges into massive folds. As the layers of rock are squeezed, the folds become more exaggerated.

▲ **Anatomy of a fold**
Geologists describe an upfold as an anticline, and a downfold as a syncline. The dip is the direction the fold is sloping. The angle of dip is how steep the slope is. The strike is the line along the fold. The axial plane is an imaginary line through the middle of the fold – this may be vertical, horizontal, or at any angle in between.

YOU WILL NEED
thin rug

Simple folds

1 Find an uncarpeted floor, and lay the rug down with one short, straight edge up against a wall. Make sure the long edge of the rug is at a right angle to the wall.

2 Now push the outer edge of the rug toward the wall. See how the rug crumples. This is how rock layers buckle to form mountains, as tectonic plates push against each other.

3 Push the rug up against the wall even more, and you will see some of the folds turn right on top of each other. These are like folded-over strata or layers, called nappes.

Complex folds

YOU WILL NEED

rolling pin, non-hardening modelling
material in various shades,
modelling tool, two blocks of
5cm/2in square wood, two bars
of 10 x 5cm/4 x 2in wood.

1 Roll out the modelling material into flat sheets in different shades, each about 5mm/¼in thick. Cut into strips about the same width as the woodblocks. Square off the ends.

2 Lay the strips carefully on top of each other, in alternating hues or in a series of hues. These strips represent the layers or strata of rock.

3 Place the woodblocks at either end of the strips. Lay the bars of wood down on either side of the strips to prevent them from twisting sideways.

5 From time to time, stop and pull the bars of wood away, so that you can have a look at what is happening. As you push harder, see how the layers crumple increasingly and start to turn over themselves. Overlapping folds like this are called nappes.

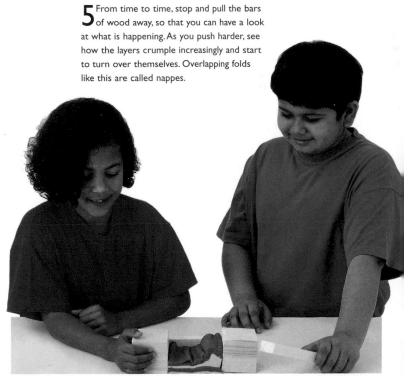

4 Ask a friend to hold on to one block, while you push the other towards it. As you push, the effect is similar to two tectonic plates slowly pushing together.

Fire down below

Volcanoes begin many kilometres/miles beneath the Earth's surface. The landscape that makes up the surface of our planet is only a thin "crust" of hard rock compared with what lies beneath. First, there is a thick layer of semiliquid rock called the mantle. Then comes an intensely hot core of iron and nickel. This reaches temperatures of 3,700°C/6,700°F, but the surrounding pressure is so great it cannot melt.

Heat moves out from the core to the mantle. Here, rocks are semiliquid and move like thick honey. They cannot melt completely because of pressure.

In some parts of the upper mantle, though, rocks do melt and are called magma. This collects in chambers, and it may bubble up through gaps in the crust via a volcano. You can watch how solids such as magma react to heat – become soft, then melt, and finally flow – in this project.

Most of the world's volcanoes lie along fault lines, where plates (sections of the Earth's crust) meet. A few, however, such as those in Hawaii, lie over hot spots beneath the Earth's crust. A hot spot is an area on a plate where hot rock from the mantle bubbles up underneath. The plate above moves, but the hot spot stays in the same place in the mantle. The hot spot keeps burning through the plate to make a volcano in a new place. A string of inactive (dead) volcanoes is left behind, as the plate moves over the hot spot. Some form islands above the ocean surface. Others, called sea mounts, remain submerged.

inner core · **outer core** · **mantle** · **crust** · **ocean** · **continent**

▲ **Inside the Earth**

Our planet is made up of different layers. The top layer is the hard crust. It is thinnest under the oceans, where it is only about 5–10km/3–6 miles thick. Underneath the crust is a thick layer of semiliquid rock called the mantle. Beneath the mantle is a layer of liquid metal, mainly iron and nickel, that makes up the Earth's outer core. The inner core at the middle is solid, and is made up of iron and other metals.

chains of dead volcanoes

active volcano

ocean plate · hot spot

Volcano chain ▶
Magma breaks through the surface plate. As the plate moves, a new part moves over the hot spot. A new volcano forms and the old one dies.

Magma temperature

YOU WILL NEED

solid margarine, jam jar,
jug (pitcher), hot water, large mixing
bowl, stopwatch.

1 Make sure the jar is clean and dry. Scoop out some margarine and drop it on to the bottom of the jar. For the best results, use solid margarine, rather than a soft margarine spread.

2 Pick up the jar and tilt it slightly. See what happens to the margarine. The answer is, not very much. It sticks to the bottom of the jar and does not slide down.

3 Fill the jug with hot water and pour some into the bowl. Shake it around to heat the bowl, then pour it out. Now pour the rest of the hot water into the bowl.

4 Pick up the jar and tilt it again. The margarine still will not move. Now place the jar on the bottom of the bowl. Keep your fingers well clear of the hot water.

5 Start the stopwatch, and after one minute, take out the jar. Tilt it and see if the margarine moves. Return it to the bowl, and after another minute, look at it again.

6 Continue checking the jar for a few more minutes. After even a minute, the margarine will slide along the bottom as it warms and starts to melt. After several minutes, it is very fluid. Rocks in the upper mantle of the Earth react to heat in a similar way as the margarine.

Moving magma

The temperature of the rocks in the Earth's mantle can be as high as 1,500°C/2,700°F. At this temperature, the rocks would usually melt, but they are under such pressure from the rocks above them that they cannot melt completely. However they are able to flow slowly. This is rather like the solid piece of modelling material in the experiment below, which flows slightly when you put enough pressure on it. This kind of flow is called plastic flow. In places, the rocks in the upper part of the mantle do melt completely. This melted rock, called

▲ **Surprise eruption**
Mount St Helens, in the north-east USA, lies in a mountain range that includes many volcanoes. Until 1980, Mount St Helens had not erupted in 130 years.

magma, collects in huge pockets called magma chambers. The magma rises because it is hotter and lighter than the semi-liquid rocks. Volcanoes form above magma chambers when the hot magma can rise to the surface. The second project demonstrates this principle using hot and cold water.

◀ **Flowing like rock**
Underneath the Earth's hard crust, the rock is semi-liquid and moves slowly. It flows in currents. Hot rock moves upward and cooler rock sinks down.

YOU WILL NEED
non-hardening modelling material,
wooden board.

Plastic flow

I Make sure that the table is protected by a sheet. Knead the lump of modelling material in your hands until it is soft and flexible. Make it into a ball and place on the table.

2 Place the board on top, and press it down. The modelling material flattens and squeezes out. It is just like semiliquid rock flowing under pressure. Make it into a ball again.

3 Press it with the board. Push the board forward at the same time. The modelling material will flow and allow the board to move forward like the plates in the Earth's crust.

Rising magma

1 Pour some of the food dye into the small jar. You may need to add more later, to give your solution a deep hue. This will make the last stage easier to see.

2 Fill the small jug with water from the hot tap. Pour it into the small jar. Fill it up to the brim, but don't let it overflow. Wipe off any water that spills down the sides.

Watch what happens. The dyed hot water begins rising from the holes. This happens because the hot water is lighter, or less dense, than the cold water around it. Magma also rises because it is less dense than the semi-liquid rock surrounding it.

3 Cut a circular piece from the plastic food wrapping a few centimetres/inches bigger than the top of the small jar. Place it over the top and secure it with the rubber band.

4 With the sharp end of the pencil, carefully make two small holes in the plastic that is covering the top of the jar. If any dyed water splashes out, wipe it off.

5 Now place the small jar inside the larger one. Use oven gloves because it is hot. Fill the large jug with cold water, and pour it into the large jar, not into the small one.

Erupting volcanoes

Volcanoes are places where molten (liquid) rock pushes up from below through splits in the Earth's crust. The word volcano comes from Vulcan, the name of the ancient Roman god of fire. Vulcanology is the term given to the study of volcanoes, and the scientists who study them are known as vulcanologists.

People usually think of volcanoes as producing molten rock. But volcanoes emit much more than just lava. The hot rock inside volcanoes produces many kinds of gases, such as steam and carbon dioxide. Some of these gases go into the air outside the volcano, and some are mixed with the lava that flows from it. The project opposite shows you how to make a volcano that throws out lava mixed with carbon dioxide. As you will see, the red, floury lava from your volcano comes out frothing, full of bubbles of this gas. In a real volcano, it is the gas that is mixed with the lava that makes the volcano suddenly explode.

▲ **Spectacular explosion**
This gigantic volcano has erupted with explosive violence. Huge clouds of rock and ash have been blasted into the air and rivers of red-hot lava cascade down its slopes. Explosive volcanoes have magma inside them that is full of gas. Gas bubbles swell inside the volcano and violently push out a mixture of lava and gas.

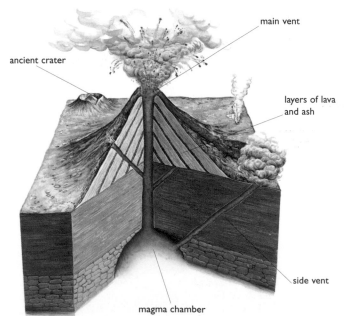

main vent

ancient crater

layers of lava and ash

side vent

magma chamber

◀ **Forming a cone**
When an explosive volcano erupts, magma (red-hot, molten rock) forces its way to the Earth's surface. It shoots into the air along with clouds of ash and gas, and runs out over the sides of the volcano. In time, layers of ash and lava build up to form a huge cone shape. Quiet volcanoes (those that do not explode because their magma contains very little gas) form a different shape.

Eruption

YOU WILL NEED

jug (pitcher), bicarbonate of soda (baking soda), flour, stirrer, funnel, plastic bottle, sand, seed tray (without holes), large plastic tray, vinegar, red food dye.

1 Make sure the jug is dry, or the mixture will stick to the sides. Empty the bicarbonate of soda into the jug and add the flour. Mix the two thoroughly using the stirrer.

2 Place the funnel in the neck of the plastic bottle. Again, first make sure that the funnel is perfectly dry. Now pour the mixture of soda and flour from the jug.

3 Empty sand into the tray until it is half full. Fill the jug with water and pour it into the tray to make the sand sticky, but not too wet. Mix together with the stirrer.

4 Stand the bottle containing the flour and soda mixture in the middle of the plastic tray. Then start packing the wet sand around it. Pat the sand into a cone shape.

The sandy volcano you have made will begin to erupt. The vinegar and soda mix to give off carbon dioxide. This makes the flour turn frothy, and forces it out of the bottle as red lava.

5 Pour the vinegar into the jug. Then add enough food dye to make the vinegar a rich red. White wine vinegar will make a richer red than malt vinegar.

6 Place the funnel in the mouth of the plastic bottle, and quickly pour into it the red vinegar in the jug. Now remove the funnel from the bottle.

Volcanic shapes

Some parts of the world have ancient lava (molten rock) flows that are hundreds of kilometres/miles long. Flows such as these have come from fissures (cracks) in the crust, which have poured out runny lava. This lava is much thinner than the lava produced by explosive volcanoes, which is sometimes called pasty lava. Scientists use the term viscosity to talk about how easily a liquid flows. Thin, runny liquids have a low viscosity, and thick liquids a high viscosity. The project shows the viscosities of two liquids, and how quickly they flow.

Heating solids to a sufficiently high temperature makes them melt and flow. Rock is no exception to this rule. Deep inside a volcano, hot rock becomes liquid and flows out on to the surface as lava. Its temperature can be as high as 1,200°C/2,200°F. Volcanoes grow in various shapes, depending on how runny or thick the lava is.

Submarine (undersea) volcanoes may grow in size until they rise above the surface of the sea.

Fissure volcanoes are giant cracks in the ground from which lava flows.

Shield volcanoes have runny lava and gentle slopes.

Vulcanian volcanoes produce thick, sticky lava and erupt with violent explosions.

Strombolian volcanoes spit out lava bombs in small explosions.

Plinian volcanoes produce thick, gassy lava and shoot columns of ash high into the air.

Lava viscosity

1 Mark a large circle on each plate by drawing around the edge of a saucer. Pour a tablespoon of honey from the jar into the middle of one of the circles. Start the stopwatch.

2 After 30 seconds, mark with the pen how far the honey has run. After another 30 seconds mark again. Stop the watch when the honey has reached the circle.

3 Part-fill the jug with dishwashing detergent and pour some into the middle of the other plate. Use the same amount as the honey you poured. Start the stopwatch.

After 30 seconds, note how far the liquid has run. You will probably find that it has already reached the circle. It flows faster because it has a much lower viscosity than honey.

◀ Fast-flowing river

A river of molten lava flows down the slopes of the volcano Kilauea on the main island of Hawaii. Like the other volcanoes on the island, Kilauea is a shield volcano. It pours out very runny lava that flows for long distances, usually at speeds up to about 100m/330ft an hour. The fastest lava flows are called by their Hawaiian name of pahoehoe.

Vicious gases

The experiments here look at two effects that the gases given out by volcanoes can have. In the first project, you can see how the build up of gas pressure can inflate a balloon. If you have put too much gas-making mixture in the bottle, the balloon may explode. Be careful! When the gas pressure builds up inside a volcano, an enormous explosion takes place, often releasing a deadly, hot gas cloud.

Volcanoes often give out the gas carbon dioxide. This is heavier than air, so a cloud of carbon dioxide descends, pushing air out of the way. Carbon dioxide can kill people and animals. They suffocate, because the cloud of carbon dioxide has replaced the air, so oxygen cannot reach their lungs. The second project shows the effect of carbon dioxide. The candle needs oxygen to burn, just as we need it to breathe. Carbon dioxide replaces the air, so the candle goes out.

▲ **Blast off**
An enormous cloud of thick ash billows from the top of Mount St. Helens, in Washington. The volcano erupted on May 18, 1980. The ash cloud rose to a height of more than 20km/12½ miles.

YOU WILL NEED
---
funnel, soft drink bottle, bicarbonate of soda (baking soda), vinegar, jug (pitcher), balloon.

The balloon starts to blow up, because of the pressure, or force, of the gas in the bottle. The more gas there is, the more the balloon fills. Don't pop the balloon!

Gas pressure

1 Place the funnel in the top of the bottle, and pour in some bicarbonate of soda. Make sure the funnel is dry or the soda will stick to it. Pour the vinegar into the bottle using the funnel.

2 Remove the funnel. Quickly fit the neck of the balloon over the top of the bottle. Notice that the vinegar and soda are fizzing as they give off bubbles of gas.

Suffocating gas

1 Place the funnel in the bottle and add the bicarbonate of soda. Pour the vinegar in from the jug. This bottle is your gas generator. The gas produced is carbon dioxide.

2 Knead a piece of modelling material until it is soft, then push it into the mouth of the bottle. Make sure it fits tightly. This will keep the gas from escaping.

5 Direct the straw of your gas generator into the bottom of the jar. Keep your arms well away from the candle flames. Soon you will find that the short candle goes out. The carbon dioxide gas has covered it and blocked out the oxygen that would have let it burn.

3 Make a hole in the clay stopper with the pencil. Carefully push the straw through the hole, so that it hangs down into the bottle. Press the modelling material around the straw.

4 Stand both candles in the bottom of the large jar. Ask an adult to light them. Light the short one first, to avoid the danger of being burned if the tall candle were lit first.

▲ A record of the past

Gas killed many of the victims at the Roman town of Pompeii. In AD79 Pompeii was buried by avalanches of hot ash and rock from the erupting Vesuvius. Archaeologists have recreated the shapes of people and animals who died there. They filled hollows left by the bodies with wet plaster of Paris and let it harden. Then they removed the cast from the lava that had covered the bodies.

Steaming hot

In some places in the world, often near plate boundaries, there is magma (hot molten rock) very near to the Earth's surface. This causes other volcanic features such as geysers and hot springs, called geothermal features. The word comes from geo, meaning the Earth, and thermal, meaning heat.

Water from the Earth's surface trickles down through holes and cracks in the land. Geothermal features are almost always caused by magma that affect underground water. The most spectacular geothermal feature is the geyser. This is a fountain of steam and water that erupts from holes in the ground. Vents (holes) called fumaroles, where steam escapes gently, are more common. Geysers and fumaroles may also give out carbon dioxide and sulfurous fumes.

Hot water can also mix with cooler water to create a hot spring, or with mud to form a bubbling mud hole. Water becomes heated in underground rocks to a temperature above body heat (about 37°C/98.6°F). Some hot springs can be twice this hot. Many are rich in minerals. For centuries, people have believed that bathing in these springs is good for health.

The first experiment on the opposite page shows you how to make a geyser using air pressure to force out water. Blowing into the top of the bottle increases the air pressure there. This forces the dyed water out of the bottle through the long straw. In the second project, you can create a mud hole and discover the sort of bubbles that form in them.

> ### YOU WILL NEED
>
> **Geyser eruption:** non-hardening modelling material, 3 bendable straws, jug (pitcher), food dye, large plastic bottle, large jar.
>
> **Mudbaths:** cornflour (cornstarch), unsweetened cocoa powder, mixing bowl, wooden spoon, measuring cup, milk, pan, oven glove.

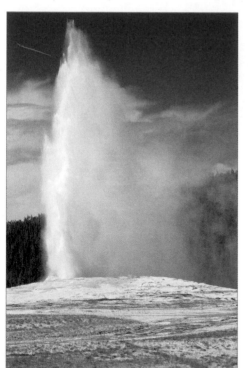

◀ Regular show
One of the most famous geysers in the world is Old Faithful, in Yellowstone National Park in Wyoming. This geyser erupts regularly about once every 45 minutes. Yellowstone is the most significant geothermal region in the USA. The National Park also boasts the world's tallest geyser, known as Steamboat. Its spouting column has been known to reach more than 115m/380ft.

Geyser eruption

1 Make two holes in a little ball of modelling material and push two bendable straws through it, as shown. Push another straw through the end of one of the first two straws.

2 Pour water into the jug and add the dye. Then pour it into the bottle. Push the stopper into the neck, so that the elongated straw dips into the dyed water.

3 Place the jar under the other end of the elongated straw, and blow into the other straw. Water spurts into the jar. If the long straw was upright, the water would spout upward like a geyser.

Mudbaths

1 Mix together 30ml/2 tbsp of cornflour and two of cocoa powder in the bowl, using the wooden spoon. Stir the mixture thoroughly until it is evenly blended.

2 Pour about 300ml/10fl oz of milk into the pan, and heat it slowly with adult supervision. Keep the ring on a low setting, to make sure the milk does not boil. Do not leave it unattended.

3 Add some cold milk, bit by bit, to the mixture of cornflour and cocoa in the bowl. Stir vigorously until the mixture has become a thick smooth cream.

4 Carefully pour the mixture into the hot milk in the pan. Hold the handle of the pan with the oven glove, and stir to stop the liquid from sticking to the bottom of the pan.

5 If you have prepared your flour and cocoa mixture well, you will now have a smooth, hot liquid that looks something like liquid mud. Soon it will start sending up thick bubbles.

The thick bubbles in the mixture will pop with gentle, plopping sounds. This is exactly what happens in hot mud pools in volcanic areas.

Volcanic rocks

The lava that flows out of volcanoes eventually cools, hardens, and becomes solid rock. Different types of lava form different kinds of rocks.

In the first project, we see how keeping a liquid under pressure stops gas from escaping. The magma (molten rock) in volcanoes usually has a lot of gas dissolved in it. As it rises through the volcano, the gases start to expand. They help push the magma up and out if the vent is clear. If the vent is blocked, the gas pressure builds up and eventually causes the volcano to explode. The lava that comes from volcanoes with gassy magma forms rock riddled with holes. In some explosive volcanoes, the lava contains so much gas that it forms pumice. This rock is so frothy and light that it floats on water.

When rising magma becomes trapped underground, it forces its way into gaps in the rocks and between the rock layers. This process is known as intrusion, and it is demonstrated by the second project. The rocks that form when the magma cools and solidifies are called intrusive rocks. Granite is the most common intrusive rock. Often, the heat of the intruding magma changes the surrounding rocks. They turn into metamorphic (changed form) rocks.

> ### YOU WILL NEED
>
> **Dissolved gas:** small jar with tight-fitting lid, bowl, jug (pitcher), antacid tablets.
>
> **Igneous intrusions:** plastic jar, bradawl, pieces of broken tiles, non-hardening modelling material, tube of toothpaste.

Sedimentary rocks, such as sandstone, form from the fragments of other rocks that have been broken down by the action of rain, snow, ice and air. These fragments are carried far away by wind or water, and settle in a different place.

At some hot parts of the Earth beneath the crust, huge pockets of liquid rock (magma) form. The magma rises, cools and solidifies to form igneous rocks such as granite. If magma reaches the surface of the Earth, it erupts as lava.

Within the Earth, the heat and pressure sometimes become so great that the surrounding rocks are changed. The new rocks are called metamorphic rocks. Marble is formed this way. It comes from limestone rock.

Dissolved gas

1 Stand the jar in the bowl. Pour cold water into the jar from the jug until the jar is nearly full to the top. Break up two antacid tablets and drop them into the jar.

2 Quickly screw the lid on the jar. Little bubbles will start to rise from the tablets, but will soon stop. Pressure has built up in the jar, and this prevents any more gas from escaping.

3 Now quickly unscrew the lid from the jar and see what happens. The whole jar starts fizzing. Removing the lid releases the pressure, and the gas in the liquid bubbles out.

Igneous intrusions

1 Make a hole in the bottom of the plastic jar with a bradawl, big enough to fit the neck of the toothpaste tube in. Keep your steadying hand away from the sharp end of the bradawl.

2 Place the pieces of broken tiles on the bottom of the jar. Keep them as flat as possible. They are supposed to represent the layers of rocks that are found in the Earth's crust.

3 Flatten out the modelling material into a disk as wide as the inside of the jar. Put the disk of modelling material inside the jar. Push it down firmly on top of the tiles.

4 Unscrew the top of the toothpaste tube, and force the neck into the hole you have made in the bottom of the bottle. You may have to widen it a little to get the neck in.

5 Squeeze the toothpaste tube. You will see the toothpaste pushing, or intruding, into the tile layers and making the disk on top rise. Molten magma often behaves in the same way. It intrudes into rock layers and makes the Earth's surface bulge.

Making crystals

Everything around you is made up of tiny particles called atoms. Crystals consist of atoms that are arranged in a regular repeating pattern. This gives the crystal its fixed outer shape. Most solid substances, including metals and minerals found in rocks, are in crystal form.

Igneous rocks are usually made of crystals that form as hot magma (molten rock) cools and solidifies. Crystals may also grow when a water solution containing minerals on the surface of the Earth evaporates. These two ways are demonstrated in the first two experiments.

The type of crystals that form depend on the substances that are dissolved in the liquid. Each mineral forms crystals with a characteristic shape. You can compare the crystals from the first two projects, which use two different solutions. The final experiment demonstrates how atoms are arranged in a crystal. In a liquid, the atoms are loosely joined together and can move around, which is why a liquid flows. As a liquid solidifies, the atoms join together in a regular pattern, like a pyramid, to form a crystal. When atoms are arranged in a disorderly way, they produce a gas.

▲ Making crystals
Place a drop of water on a small, dry mirror and then put it in the freezer. The water will freeze into crystals, which can be seen with a magnifying glass.

YOU WILL NEED
water, measuring cup, pan, sugar, tablespoon, wooden spoon, glass jar.

Growing crystals from sugar solution

1 Ask an adult to heat 600ml/1 pint/ 2½ cups of water in a pan until it is hot, but not boiling. Using a tablespoon, add sugar to the hot water until no more sugar will dissolve in the solution.

2 Stir the solution well, then allow it to cool. When it is completely cold, pour the solution from the pan into a glass jar, and put it somewhere where it will not be disturbed.

After a few days or weeks, the solution starts to evaporate and the sugar in the solution will gradually begin to form crystals. The longer it is undisturbed, the larger your crystals will grow.

Growing crystals from sodium carbonate

1 Get an adult to pour 250ml/8fl oz/ 1 cup very hot water into a jug. Add a spoonful of sodium carbonate. Stir until it all dissolves. Add more sodium carbonate until no more will dissolve.

2 Dissolving a solid in a liquid makes a solution. Your solution is said to be saturated, because no more solid will dissolve. Pour the solution into a bowl, leaving undissolved solids in the jug.

3 A crystal needs somewhere to start growing. Use a piece of thread to attach the paper clip to the straw. The distance from straw to clip should be about two-thirds the depth of the bowl.

4 Balance the straw on top of the bowl to let the paper clip dangle in the water. As time goes by, water evaporates, leaving crystals on the paper clip.

5 After several days, remove the clip and crystals from the solution, and wash them under the cold tap. Look at the crystals through a magnifying glass. The shapes of your crystals are identical.

Make a model crystal

1 Fit a layer of blue marbles into the tray in a square pattern. Each central atom is surrounded by eight others. (In some substances, atoms are arranged in a hexagon – a six-sided shape.)

2 Add a second layer. Each marble sits in a dip between four marbles in the layer below. Add a third layer. Each marble is directly above a marble in the first layer.

3 Add two more layers of marbles to make up a complete model crystal. The model crystal you have made is the shape of a square pyramid, because you used a square tray.

Glass and bubbles

Igneous rocks begins deep within the Earth as magma (molten rock). The word igneous means "of fire". Magma rises toward the surface where it may erupt as lava from a volcano, or cool and solidify within the Earth's crust as igneous rock. Rocks formed in this way are a mass of interlocking crystals, which makes them very strong and ideal as building stones.

The size of the crystals in an igneous rock depends on how quickly the magma cooled. Lavas that cool quickly contain very small crystals. Basalt and andesite are two common kinds of fine-grained igneous rocks, with small crystals. Other rocks, such as granite, cooled more slowly because they solidified inside the Earth's crust. These have a grainy texture because the crystals had time to grow.

The experiments opposite show how igneous rocks can be grainy or smooth and glassy. They use sugar to represent magma. Sugar melts at a low enough temperature for you to experiment with, but it will still be very hot, so ask an adult to help you do these projects. To make real magma, you would need to heat rock up to around 1,000°C/1,830°F until it melted! You can also make the sugar solution into bubbly honeycomb, a form similar to pumice stone.

▲ Basalt
Dark, heavy basalt is one of the most common volcanic rocks. It is formed from the thin, runny lava that pours out of some volcanoes. This sample is called vesicular basalt because it is riddled with vesicles (holes).

▲ Andesite
Lava from explosive volcanoes is thicker and less runny. It can form andesite, which is less dark than basalt. Andesite is so-called because it is the typical rock found in the Andes Mountains in Peru.

honeycomb (pumice)   toffee (obsidian)

fudge (granite)

▲ Pumice
The bubbles in honeycomb are like those in pumice. Pumice is a very light rock that is full of holes. It forms when lava that contains a lot of gas pours out of underwater volcanoes.

▲ Obsidian
Glassy toffee cools too rapidly to form crystals. Obsidian is a volcanic rock that is formed when lava cools very quickly. It looks like black glass and is often called volcanic glass.

▲ Granite
Fudge's grainy texture is similar to granite. The crystals are large, because they grew slowly as the magma cooled slowly. Rhyolite is a kind of granite with smaller crystals and sharp edges.

Crystalline rock

1 Ask an adult to heat 500g/1¼lb/ 2½ cups of sugar with a little water in a pan. Continue heating until the mixture turns brown, but not black, then add a splash of milk. Leave to cool.

2 After an hour, you should see tiny crystal grains in the fudge mixture. Once it is completely cool, feel its grainy texture in your hands. The texture is similar to granite.

Glass and bubbles

1 Use waxed paper to spread the butter on a metal baking tray. Put it in the freezer for at least an hour to get cold. Use oven gloves to take the tray from the freezer.

2 Ask an adult to heat about 500g/ 2½ cups of sugar with a little water in a pan. The sugar dissolves in the water, but the water soon evaporates, leaving only sugar.

3 Stir the sugar mixture with a wooden spoon while it is heating. Make sure that the sugar does not burn and turn black. It should be golden brown.

4 Pour the mixture on to the cool baking tray. After 10 minutes, the glassy and brittle toffee will be cool enough to pick up. Like obsidian, toffee cools too rapidly to form crystals.

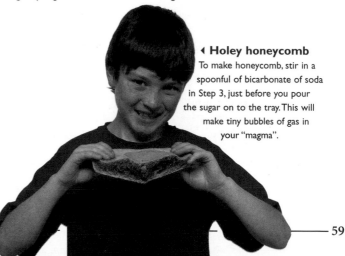

◀ **Holey honeycomb**
To make honeycomb, stir in a spoonful of bicarbonate of soda in Step 3, just before you pour the sugar on to the tray. This will make tiny bubbles of gas in your "magma".

Layers on layers

Many of the most familiar rocks around us are sedimentary rocks. Particles of rock, shells and bones of sea creatures settle in layers, and then harden into rock over thousands of years. Rock particles form when other rocks are eroded (worn down) by the weather and are carried away by wind, rivers, and ice sheets. They become sediments when they are dumped and settle. Sediments may collect in river deltas, lakes and the sea. Large particles make conglomerates (large pebbles cemented together), medium ones make sandstones, and fine particles make clays.

To understand the processes by which sedimentary rocks are made, and how they form distinct layers called strata, you can make your own sedimentary rocks. Different strata of rock are laid down by different types of sediment, so the first project involves making strata using various things found in the kitchen. The powerful forces that move parts of the Earth's crust often cause strata to fold, fault or just tilt, and you can see this, too. In the second project, you can make a type of sedimentary rock called a conglomerate, in which sand cements pebbles together.

▲ Cracks in the rockface
Once they have formed, sedimentary rocks may be subject to powerful forces caused by the movement of the Earth's crust. Splits in the ground reveal how this strata has folded and cracked.

YOU WILL NEED
large jar, non-hardening modelling material, spoon, flour, kidney beans, soft dark brown sugar, rice, lentils (or a similar variety of ingredients of different tones and textures).

Your own strata

I Press one edge of a large jar into a piece of modelling material, so that the jar sits at an angle. Slowly and carefully spoon a layer of flour about 2cm/¾in thick into the jar.

2 Carefully add layers of kidney beans, brown sugar, rice, lentils and flour, building them up until they almost reach the top of the jar. Try to keep the side of the jar clean.

3 Remove the jar from the clay and stand it upright. The different toned and textured layers are like a section through a sequence of natural sedimentary rocks.

Making conglomerate rock

1 Put on a pair of rubber gloves. In an old plastic container, make up some plaster of Paris with water, following the instructions on the packet. Stir with a fork or spoon.

2 Before the plaster starts to harden, mix some small pebbles, sand, and earth into the plaster of Paris. Stir the mixture thoroughly, to make sure it is all evenly distributed.

3 Leave the mixture for 10 minutes, until the plaster begins to harden, then take a small lump of it in your hand and form it into a ball shape to look like conglomerate rock.

4 Make more conglomerate rocks in different sizes containing different amounts of pebbles. Place the rocks on a spare piece of paper so that they can harden and dry out completely.

▲ Natural cement

Conglomerates in nature can be found in areas that were once under water. Small pebbles and shells become rounded and cemented together by the water.

◀ Clues in the cutaway

The 1.6km/1 mile-deep Grand Canyon, in Arizona, was cut by the Colorado River. The cliff face reveals strata (layers of rock). The strata at the bottom are more than two billion years old. Those at the top are about 60 million years old. Each layer is a different type of rock, suggesting that conditions in this region changed many times in the past. For this reason, sedimentary rock strata can provide valuable clues about the distant history of the Earth.

What's a fossil?

The remains of some plants and animals that died long ago can be seen in rock as fossils. After an animal dies, it may become buried in sediments – rock particles ground down by wind and water. Slowly, over thousands of years, the sediments compact together to form sedimentary rock. The shape or outline of the plant or animal is preserved.

The study of fossils, called palaeontology, tells us much about how life evolved, both in the sea and on the land. Fossils give clues to the type of environment in which an organism lived, and can also help to date rocks.

These projects will help you to understand how two types of fossil came to exist. One type forms when sediment settles around a dead animal or plant. It hardens to rock, and the plant or animal rots away. This space in the rock is an outline of the dead animal or plant. This is usually how the soft parts of an animal, or a delicate leaf, are preserved. You can make this kind of fossil using a shell. In this case the shell does not decay – you simply remove it from the plaster.

The second project shows you another kind of fossil. Here, the skeleton of a decaying animal is filled with minerals. The minerals gradually become rock. This gives a solid fossil that is a copy of the original body part.

fern

ammonite

▲ **Turned to stone**

Two common fossils are shown here. Fossils of sea creatures are often found, because their bodies cannot decay completely underwater. Ammonites were hard-shelled sea creatures that lived between 60 million and 400 million years ago. Fernlike fossils are often found in coal.

YOU WILL NEED

Fossil imprint: safety glasses, plastic container, plaster of Paris, water, fork, strip of paper, paper clip, non-hardening modelling material, shell, wooden board, hammer, chisel.

Solid fossil: spare paper, rolling pin, modelling material, shell, petroleum jelly, paper clip, strip of paper, glass jar, plaster of Paris, water, fork.

How fossils are formed

An animal or plant dies. Its body falls on to the sand at the bottom of the ocean, or into mud on land. If it is buried quickly, then the body is protected from being eaten.

The soft parts of the body rot away, but the bones and teeth remain. After a long time, the hard parts are replaced by minerals – usually calcite, but sometimes pyrite or quartz.

After millions of years, the rocks in which the fossils formed are eroded and exposed again. Some fossils look as fresh now as the day when the plant or animal was first buried.

Fossil imprint

1 In a plastic container, mix up the plaster of Paris with some water. Follow the instructions on the packet. Make sure the mixture is fairly firm and not too runny.

2 Make a collar out of a strip of paper fastened with a paper clip. Use modelling material to make a base to fit under the collar. Press the shell into the clay. Surround the shell with plaster.

3 Leave your plaster rock to dry for at least half an hour. Crack open the rock and remove the shell. You will then see the imprint left behind after the shell has gone.

Solid fossil

1 Put a spare piece of paper down on your work surface to protect it. Using the rolling pin, roll out some modelling material into a flat circle, about 2cm/¾in thick.

2 Press your shell, or another object with a distinctive shape, deep into the clay to leave a clear impression. Do not press it all the way to the paper at the bottom.

3 Remove the shell and lightly rub some petroleum jelly over the clay circle, which is now the shell mould. This will help you to remove the plaster fossil later.

4 Use the paper clip to fasten the paper strip into a collar for the mould. Mix up some plaster of Paris according to the instructions, pour it in, and leave it to set for half an hour.

5 Remove the solid plaster from the mould. In order not to damage them, palaeontologists have to remove fossilized bones or teeth, from rock or earth, very carefully.

These are the finished results of the two projects. Real fossils are imprints of organisms that lived millions of years ago.

Hard as nails!

The best way to learn about rocks is to look closely at as many different types as you can find. Look at pebbles on the beach and the stones in your garden. You will find that they are not all the same. Collect specimens of different pebbles and compare them. Give each stone an identification number and record where you found it, and its characteristics. A magnifying glass will help you see more details than can be seen with the naked eye. Look for different tones, shapes and hardness. Ask an adult to take you to a geological museum to compare your stone with the specimens there.

You can try simple versions of tests that geologists use on the following pages. They will help you identify some samples that you have collected. The first test involves rubbing a rock on to the back of a tile to leave a streak mark. The colour of the streak can give a clue to what minerals are present in the rock. The second test shows you how to discover a rock's hardness, by seeing how easily a mineral scratches. Hardness is measured on a scale devised in 1822 by Friedrich Mohs. He made a list of ten common minerals called Mohs' scale, which runs from 1 (the softest) to 10 (the hardest). The hardest natural mineral is diamond, with a hardness of 10. It will scratch all other minerals.

▲ Be a detective
Clean a rock with a stiff brush and some water. Stand in plenty of light and experiment to find the correct distance to see the rock's details clearly with a magnifying glass.

beach pebbles

▲ Wearing away
Look at the different sizes of pebbles on a beach. The constant to-and-fro of the waves grinds the pebbles smaller and smaller. Eventually these particles will form sedimentary rock.

◀ Hidden inside
When mineral-rich water fills a crack or cavity in a rock, veins and geodes form. A geode is a rounded rock, with a hollow middle lined with crystals. The beautiful crystal lining is revealed when it is split open. Geodes are highly prized by mineral collectors.

outside of geode

inside of geode

quartz

copper

▲ What is a mineral?
All rocks are made up of one or more minerals. Minerals, such as copper and quartz, are natural, solid, nonliving substances. Each mineral has definite characteristics, such as shape and colour, that distinguish it from other minerals.

Streak test

1 Place a tile face down, so that the rough side is facing upward. Choose one of your samples and rub it against the tile. You should see a streak appear on the tile.

2 Make streaks using the other samples and compare the colours. Rocks made of several minerals may leave several different streaks. Try to identify them in your field guide.

Testing for hardness

1 Clean some rock samples with water using a nail brush. Scratch the rocks together. On the Mohs' scale, a mineral is harder than any minerals it can make scratches on.

2 A fingernail has a hardness of just over 2. Scratch each rock with a fingernail – if it scratches the rock, the minerals out of which the rock is made have a hardness of 2 or less.

3 Put aside those rocks scratched by a fingernail. Scratch those remaining with a coin. A coin has a hardness of about 3, so minerals it scratches are less than 3.

4 Now scratch the remaining rocks on a glass jar. If any of the rocks make a scratch on the jar, then the minerals they contain must be harder than glass.

5 Put aside any rocks that will not scratch the glass. They are less hard than glass, which measures somewhere between 5 and 6. Try scratching the remainder of the rocks with a steel file (hardness 7), and finally with a sheet of sandpaper (hardness 8).

Testing for minerals

Rocks and minerals are the naturally occurring materials that make up planet Earth. Rocks are used for buildings, and many minerals are prized as jewels. Most people think of rocks as hard and heavy, but soft materials, such as sand, chalk and clay, are also considered to be rocks. Different rocks are made up from mixtures of different minerals. The minerals inside a rock form small crystals that are locked together to form a hard solid.

Geologists (scientists who study the Earth and its rocks) use many different methods to identify minerals that make up rocks. These experiments will help you to discover which minerals are in a rock sample. You can also identify rocks with a magnifying glass or from their hardness.

The acid test demonstrates if a gas is given off by the mineral. The second experiment is used to discover a rock sample's specific gravity. It compares a mineral's density to the density of water. Density measures how compact the particles are that make up a sample. Every mineral has a different density, which means that samples of the same mineral will have the same density.

▲ Weighing up the evidence
These two bricks are the same size and shape, but do not weigh the same. The materials they are made of have different densities.

YOU WILL NEED

vinegar, bowl, spoon, samples of

different stones, magnifying glass,

reference book.

Acid test

1 Pour some vinegar into a bowl. Drop rock samples into the vinegar. If gas bubbles form, then the rock contains minerals called carbonates (such as calcite).

2 Alternatively, you can put a few drops of vinegar on each rock sample. Watch them carefully for clues to what they might be. Chalk, marble and limestone make vinegar fizz.

3 Limestone reacts with vinegar. Like chalk and marble, it reacts because it is a type of calcium carbonate. Common rocks such as flint, granite and sandstone are unaffected.

flint   granite

limestone   sandstone

4 Now scratch one sample with another. Harder rocks leave marks on softer ones. Hardness also helps you to identify rocks. Think how difficult it might be to carve the harder ones.

5 Arrange your rocks in order of hardness. Igneous rocks, such as granite, are usually the hardest. Sedimentary rocks, such as sandstone, are usually the softest.

6 Use a lens to examine your rocks. There are sharp crystal minerals in igneous rocks. Metamorphic rocks look smooth and sedimentary rocks have layers and tiny bits in them.

Density or specific gravity test

YOU WILL NEED

mineral or rock samples, accurate

food scales, notebook, pen or

pencil, measuring cup, water.

1 Choose a rock or mineral sample, and weigh it as accurately as you can to find its mass. The figure should be in grams or ounces. Make a note of the mass in your notebook.

2 Fill a clear measuring cup to the 250ml/8fl oz mark with cold water. Choose your first rock or mineral sample and carefully place it in the water.

4 The new figure is the sample's volume in millilitres or fluid ounces. Now divide the mass by the volume. You can use a calculator to do this equation if you wish. This will give you the rock sample's density, or specific gravity.

3 Look at the scale on the cup to read the new water level. Make a note of the level of the water in your notebook. Now subtract 250ml/ 8fl oz from that figure.

Natural Wonders Close to Home

When forests are cut down, the plants and animal habitats that depend on the trees in those forests are put at risk. This section focuses on the natural habitats near your home, to explore the importance of plants, insects, and birds in the way nature works on Earth.

What is soil?

Soil is formed from decayed vegetable matter (dead leaves and plants), mineral grains and larger pieces of rock. Creatures, such as earthworms, help the decomposition process by mixing the soil. The process by which rocks are often broken down into smaller pieces is called weathering. Chemical weathering occurs when minerals are dissolved by water. Some minerals break down or dissolve quickly. Others, such as quartz, are not dissolved but stay behind in the soil as stones. The action of burrowing animals, insects and growing plants is called physical weathering. Attrition (grinding down) is another kind of physical weathering and it occurs when wind-blown particles rub against each other. This kind of weathering occurs mainly in dry areas, such as deserts. You can see how attrition works, simply by shaking some sugar cubes together in a glass jar.

In the first experiment, you can examine what makes up the soil. The second shows you the range of sizes of mineral and rock particles in a soil sample. In the last project, you can find out how sediments form in rivers, lakes, and seas. First large, and then finer, particles of sediment are deposited.

▲ **On the horizon**
Soil occurs in layers, called horizons. There are four main horizons. The top horizon (also known as topsoil) is a layer of fine particles that supports the roots of plants and trees. The next two layers, beneath the topsoil, have larger soil particles. The bottom layer is partly solid rock.

Wormery

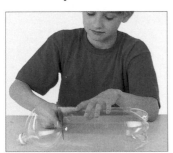

1 Cut the top off the large, clear plastic bottle, as shown. Place the smaller bottle inside the larger one. Make sure the gap is evenly spaced all the way around the smaller bottle.

2 Fill the gap with layers of soil and sand to within 5cm/2in of the top. Press the soil down lightly. Gently place the worms on top of the soil, and cover them with rotting leaves.

3 Cover the sides with black paper. Keep the soil moist. After a few days, remove the paper to see how the worms have tunneled away and dragged leaves into their burrows.

What is in soil?

1 Put on a pair of gardening gloves and place a trowel full of soil into the strainer. Shake the strainer over a piece of paper for about a minute or so.

2 Tap the side of the strainer gently, to help separate the different parts of the soil. Are there chunks that will not go through the strainer? Can you see if any of the chunks are rock?

3 Use a magnifying glass to examine the soil particles that fall on to the paper. Are there any small creatures or mineral grains? Make a note of what you see in your notebook.

YOU WILL NEED

Wormery: large and small plastic bottles, scissors, funnel, gloves, damp soil, sand, six worms, rotting leaves, black paper, adhesive tape.

What is in soil?: gloves, trowel, soil, strainer, paper, magnifying glass, notebook, pen.

Big or small?: scissors, large clear plastic bottle, wooden spoon, gravel, earth, sand, water, jug (pitcher).

Big or small?

1 Use a pair of scissors to cut the top off a large, clear plastic bottle. Ask an adult to help, if you need to. You can recycle the top part of the bottle.

floating soil and plant fragments

water made cloudy by fine particles of clay

settled mineral particles

2 Use a spoon to scoop some gravel, earth and sand into the bottom of the bottle. Add water to the mixture, until it nearly reaches to the top of the bottle.

3 Stir vigorously to mix the stones, earth and sand with the water. In a river, soil and rock particles are mixed together and carried along by the moving water.

Leave the mixture to settle. You should find that the particles settle into different layers, with the heaviest particles at the bottom, and the lightest at the top.

Examining soil

Beneath the ground, the soil teems with life. Worms, slugs, millipedes and beetles live there, feeding on decaying matter. Tiny living creatures, called decomposers, break down everything that remains. Decomposers include microscopic bacteria, fungi, woodlice, mites and small insects. They digest organic material such as dead animals, leaves and plants, and break it down into nutrients. This process, called decomposition, creates a rich fertilizer for plants growing in the soil. As organic material rots, its nutrients or goodness are returned to the soil. The nutrients dissolve in rain water and trickle down to tree and other plant roots below.

The first experiment demonstrates the best conditions for decomposing plants. It shows that plant material decays quickest in warm, moist areas. You can take a closer look at the decomposers themselves in the second project, which shows how to separate creepy-crawlies from the rotting leaves they live in. You could repeat the experiment with leaves from a different area, and see if the insects you find are the same.

▲ **Feast for woodlice**
Rotting, in nature, does not happen by itself. Dead leaves are food for decomposers, such as woodlice. They eat the fallen leaves and pass many of the nutrients back into the soil, to be taken up again by the trees' roots.

Watching decay in the soil

YOU WILL NEED

gardening gloves, trowel (optional), two clean plastic containers, soil, dead leaves, water in a watering can, one container lid.

1 Be sure to wear a pair of gardening gloves for this project. Use your hand, or a trowel if you prefer, to fill two plastic containers with plenty of dry soil.

2 Put a layer of dead leaves on top of the soil in one of the containers. Water the leaves and soil thoroughly, then press the lid on to the container to cover it.

3 Place a layer of leaves on the dry soil in the other container. Do not water it and do not cover the container. Store both containers in a dry place.

After a few weeks, the leaves in the wet soil (*above left*) will have begun to rot, and those in the dry soil (*above right*) will have shrivelled.

Studying decomposers

YOU WILL NEED

plastic funnel, large clear jar, gloves, rotting leaves from a compost heap, black paper, adhesive tape, desk lamp, magnifying glass, field guide.

1 Rotting leaves are covered in insects and other creepy-crawlies. You can separate them by using a lamp, a funnel and a large jar. Put the funnel inside the jar, as shown.

2 Wearing a pair of gardening gloves, loosely fill the funnel with rotting leaves. Tape a sheet of black paper around the sides of the jar to block out the light.

After an hour, there will be several creatures in the jar. Look at them with a magnifying glass and use a field guide to identify them. Then return the creatures to where you found them.

3 Place the lamp so that it shines on the leaves. The creatures will move away from the heat and the light of the lamp, and fall down the slippery funnel into the jar below.

Tree study

There are several kinds of trees. In tropical rainforests, where it is warm and wet all year, most trees are evergreen and keep their leaves the entire year. Tropical rainforests are found near the Equator, where there is little difference between the seasons. In countries with a temperate (moderate) climate, deciduous, broad-leaved trees shed their leaves in fall. Losing leaves reduces evaporation. This helps the tree conserve energy and water when the ground water is frozen, and reduces damage by frost.

Trees can be identified by looking at such characteristics as bark, leaves and flowers, and in fall by their fruits and nuts, some of which are shown on the right. The size and shape of the trunk and branches can also help to identify a tree, and scientists record the tree's girth by measuring the distance around the trunk at chest height. You can study trees in your backyard, a local park or the wood following the same checks. Choose an area of mixed woodland with many different trees. Always take an adult with you to keep you safe.

leaf from a plane tree

seedcase from a sycamore tree

hips and leaves from a cockspur thorn tree

a chestnut and its case from a horse chestnut tree

seeds from a lime tree

acorn and its cup from an oak tree

Identifying trees

1 Walk along a path in a park or in the woods. Try to identify the trees you find there from their general height and shape. Use a field guide on trees to help you.

2 Bark can help you identify some trees. Silver birch bark is smooth and white with dark cracks. Match the bark of different trees with pictures in your guide.

3 Study leaf tones and shapes, and the fruits and seeds of trees. Learn to identify trees with the help of the field guide, and make a record of them in a notebook.

Measuring a tree's height

1 With the long ruler, measure 19m/19 yds from the tree and push the stick into the ground. Measure another 1m/1 yd from the stick and lie down straight on the ground.

2 Use one eye to line up the top of the tree with the stick. Get a friend to mark this point on the stick in the ground. The height of the tree is 20 times this distance.

Measuring a tree's girth

1 Stick a piece of adhesive tape on the end of a piece of string. Wrap the string around a tree trunk at chest height. Mark where it meets the tape with your finger.

2 Lay the string along the long ruler to find the length. This number is the girth of the tree. Measure another tree of the same species. Is its girth the same? Why might they differ?

	1 square = 2.5cm/1in
	evergreen
	beech
	horse chesnut
	cherry
	silverbirch

3 Make a chart with drawings of the different trees that you have measured. The trees with the thickest trunks are usually older than those with slender trunks.

▲ Rings of age

You can clearly see the growth rings on the trunk of this old oak tree. Each year, the tree grows a new ring of wood just under the bark.

Looking at bark

▲ Close-up view

If you look closely at the bark of a tree, you can discover many clues about its life. Plants and fungi may be clinging to the surface. There might also be insects and other tiny creatures hiding inside cracks...

The skin that covers a tree – the bark – keeps the tree from drying out and helps to protect it against attack by animals and fungi. Bark may be thin and smooth, or thick and knobbly, depending on the type of tree and its age. Young trees usually have smooth bark on their trunks and branches. Old bark stretches and cracks or peels, as the trunk grows wider year by year. Just underneath the bark is a delicate layer of tissue called phloem. It carries nutrients from the leaves to all parts of the tree. If a bark is damaged all around the tree trunk, the flow of food stops and the tree dies.

The appearance of the bark can help you decide what species (type) a tree is. Different trees have different kinds of bark. A mature beech tree has smooth, thin bark that is about 1cm/½in deep. A redwood tree of the same size has hairy, fibrous bark that is up to 15cm/6in thick. Many conifers, such as pines and spruces, have bark that flakes off. Follow the first two projects and become a bark detective, by studying the bark up close and making a collection of your own bark rubbings. The third project will help you estimate the size of a tree.

YOU WILL NEED

magnifying glass, field guide,

notebook, pencil.

Become a bark detective

1 Bark does not stretch, but cracks and peels as a tree grows. Use a magnifying glass to search in the cracks during the spring and summer for tiny insects and other creatures.

2 The bark has fallen away from this dead tree, revealing the holes chewed by beetle grubs underneath. Some grubs live under the bark for several years.

3 Where the bark is damp, you will often find powdery green patches. These are millions of microscopic plants called algae, which live side by side on the bark's surface.

Bark rubbing book

> ### YOU WILL NEED
>
> paper, wax crayons, pencil, thin
> green card, bradawl or hole
> puncher, ribbon, adhesive.

1 Ask a friend to hold a sheet of paper steady against the bark. Rub the side of a crayon over the paper with long, even strokes. Write the name of the tree beside each rubbing.

2 Punch holes into pieces of green card and bind them together with ribbon. Stick your rubbings on to each page. You could include a silhouette of each tree, too.

Measuring the crown

> ### YOU WILL NEED
>
> compass, marker, long ruler,
> graph paper, ruler,
> coloured pencils.

1 Using the compass, walk away from the tree toward north. Ask a friend to call out when you reach the edge of the area covered by the leaves. Place a marker at this point.

2 Repeat for the other seven main compass directions (NE, E, SE, S, SW, W, NW). Measure the distances back to the trunk with a long ruler and note them down.

3 Plot your results on a piece of graph paper. Measure 1cm/½in on the paper for each metre/yard on the ground. Draw lines from the middle of the paper, for each compass direction.

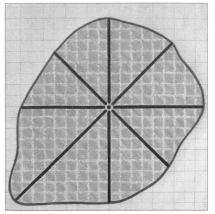

What you have sketched and filled in shows the shape of the area covered by trees leaves and branches (the crown). Count the squares and half squares to find the size of the area of the crown. Do not count part-squares if they are less than a half. Each 1cm/½in square represents 1m/1yd. Compare with other trees in the area. Generally, the older the tree, the more likely it will have a larger crown.

Specimen collection

Different kinds of trees grow naturally in different parts of the world. Where they grow depends mainly on climate. Look closely at trees in winter and you will see that even deciduous trees are not completely bare. Each twig has buds along its sides and at the tip. Buds have protective skins with tiny immature leaves and stems curled up inside. When spring sunshine warms the trees, buds begin to grow and swell. Finally, they burst open and small leaves emerge. Leaves contain pipes called veins. Water pumps into these veins, making the leaves stiffen and flatten as they grow to full size.

To learn about trees, you can make a collection of dead leaves, cones and bark from each one you study. Do not forget to look for things throughout the year – flowers and buds in spring, seeds and fruit in the fall. Label your collection.

bud scale · folded leaf · short stem

▲ Budding
Buds grow in the middle of a twig between two leaf stems. An unopened bud contains tiny leaves, and a shoot that will grow in spring and make the leaf stem longer. The illustration above shows what it looks like inside.

Tree zones

Evergreen conifer trees, such as pine and firs, usually grow where the climate is cold. Long, snowy winters are followed by short, cool summers, with moderate amounts of rain. Forests of conifers grow in a band across North America, Europe and Asia.

Broad-leaved deciduous trees, such as oak, ash, and maple, grow in temperate climates away from hot, dry tropics or the snowy poles. There are more kinds of trees than in a coniferous forest. Temperate forests are found in North America, Europe, Asia and New Zealand.

Tropical countries lie close to the Equator. The weather is hot, and daylight lasts for 12 hours a day for most of the year. Dense rainforests grow where heavy rain falls almost continuously, such as South America, Africa, Asia and Australasia.

Savanna is a dry, tropical grassland, with some shrubs and bushes. Trees grow alone, or in widely spaced small groups. Forests cannot grow because the dry season lasts most of the year. Trees that do grow here are species that can survive for long periods without water.

Collecting specimens

I How many different leaves and cones can you find? Make sure you note down the name of the tree that each specimen comes from. Start a collection with your friends.

2 To dry and flatten your leaves, place sheets of kitchen paper between the pages of a large and heavy book. Lay your leaves out on the paper on one side only. Close the book.

3 Pile more books on top. Make sure the pile cannot topple over and will not get disturbed. The weight presses the leaves flat, and the kitchen paper absorbs moisture.

4 Wait for at least one month, until the leaves are flat and dry. Glue them into your notebook, or on to sheets of thick paper, and make them into a book. Use a field guide to identify each leaf.

5 For bark specimens, only collect bark from dead trees that have fallen over. You can make bark rubbings from living trees. See page 76 for instructions on how to make rubbings.

6 Springtime flowers soon wither and die. These young horse chestnuts will last much longer. It is better to take photographs of flowers, rather than pick them.

7 You can look at young cones and leaves from the lowest branches of evergreen pines, firs and cedars. Look under these trees for cones that have fallen.

Make a large display case for your collection. You can make this from a shoe box by sticking in pieces of card to make compartments. Pressed leaves keep their shape and can last for a long time, if they are kept dry.

How plants grow

All plants need water to live. They do not take in food as animals do, but make their own using water from the ground, and carbon dioxide gas from the air. Water is absorbed through a plant's roots. It travels up through the stem or trunk into the leaves, shoots, and flowers. The water also carries the nutrients from the soil to all parts of the plant. In the leaves, nutrients and water are used for photosynthesis, the process of making energy from light. Excess water not needed by the plant evaporates back into the air in the form of water vapour in a process called transpiration. You can see how much water vapour is transpired by a plant in the first experiment.

When a seed begins to grow, we say that it has germinated. Germination occurs when conditions are warm and moist enough for the seed to swell and split its skin. A tiny root grows downward, and a thin shoot pushes upwards toward the light. The second project shows you how to germinate a seed and help it grow into a tree. Germinating a seed in this way takes about two months.

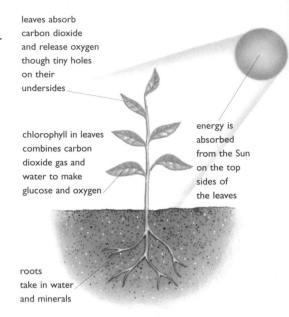

leaves absorb carbon dioxide and release oxygen though tiny holes on their undersides

chlorophyll in leaves combines carbon dioxide gas and water to make glucose and oxygen

energy is absorbed from the Sun on the top sides of the leaves

roots take in water and minerals

▲ Converting energy

Photosynthesis is the process through which plants use the water in the ground and the energy in sunlight to make their food. Leaves take in carbon dioxide and water to make oxygen and glucose (sugar). Glucose flows to all parts of the plant, supplying energy for growth. Oxygen gas escapes through the holes on the underside of the leaves. The oxygen is released back into the air. We need oxygen to breathe.

Survival in the wetlands ▸

Swamps are places where the ground is permanently waterlogged, such as in muddy river estuaries. Most trees cannot survive in swamps, because they need fresh water and air around their roots. Some types of mangroves have breathing roots that grow upwards, so that their tips are above the surface of the water. Mangrove swamps are home to kingfishers, giant water bugs, crabs, turtles, crocodiles and mudskippers, a type of fish that spends much of its time out of water.

Evaporation in action

1 Water the house plant well using a watering can. Water the plant at the base, so the roots can draw the water up. If you water the plant from the top, water just the soil, not the plant itself.

2 Place a large, transparent plastic bag over the plant, taking care not to damage the leaves. Tape the bag tightly around the pot. Leave the plant overnight.

◀ Floating water
Trees pass millions of gallons of water vapour into the air each day. The vapour forms thick clouds of tiny water droplets over the forest.

3 Look at the plant the next day. Inside the bag, water vapour given off by the plant turns back into water. The air inside is warm and moist, like the air in a rainforest.

Germinate an acorn

1 Fill the flower pot with soil mix and bury an acorn just beneath the surface. Put it in a warm place and keep the soil moist. Plant several acorns, since one may not germinate.

2 When a tiny tree starts to grow by itself, it is called a seedling. It needs light and regular watering to grow well. Do not soak the soil with water, or the roots will rot and die.

3 Your seedling should grow rapidly for a few weeks and then stop. During the winter, it will need little water. In the spring, you can take the seedling out of its pot and plant it outside.

Reaching for light

Look at a leaf and you will see that the top side is usually greener than the underside. This is because there is more chlorophyll, a green substance that traps energy from sunlight. Plants cannot move around to find food as animals do. Instead, they make their own. The green cells work like tiny solar panels, using sunlight to combine carbon dioxide gas from the air and water from the ground. The cells then produce a sugar (glucose) and oxygen gas. This process is called photosynthesis. Without light, plants cannot make their food.

Photosynthesis is the ultimate source of food on Earth, because animals eat plants or other animals that live on plants. Photosynthesis is also the source of all oxygen in our atmosphere. The projects show how plants try to reach the light. Epiphytes are special kinds of plants that do not need to grow in soil. They live on high branches in the rainforests to get closer to the light.

▲ **Catching the rays**
Trees spread their leaves widely to absorb as much energy as they can from sunlight. They use the energy to make a sugary substance called glucose. Liquids flow in and out of leaves through veins. Veins also act like ribs that help to stiffen the leaf and keep it flat.

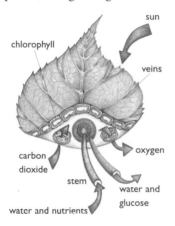

sun
chlorophyll
veins
carbon dioxide
oxygen
stem
water and glucose
water and nutrients

▲ **Making energy**
Photosynthesis happens near the top surface of a leaf, where sunlight has the strongest impact.

Grow your own epiphyte

1 Put on a pair of gloves to protect your hands. Wrap moss around one end of the branch or a piece of driftwood. Tie the moss securely in place with thread.

2 Pile some gravel into a sturdy plant pot, until the pot is almost full. It needs to be almost full to support the wood. You could use a trowel to help you transfer the gravel.

3 Now push the branch or driftwood down into the gravel, until it stands up in the pot without tipping it over. Use a water spray to spray the moss with water.

4 Arrange the epiphytes (available from garden stores) by pressing them gently into the moss. A drop of glue on the base of each plant will help to hold it in place.

5 Remember to spray the epiphytes from time to time with water. You could also add a few drops of liquid plant food, to help the epiphytes to grow.

Epiphytes grow well indoors and make an unusual display. They do not need soil to grow. Instead they wrap their roots around a branch.

Searching for the light

1 Watch a plant search for the light as it grows, by making a maze. Cut a hole in the end of a shoe box and stick eight flaps of cardboard inside with adhesive tape, as shown here.

2 Paint the inside of the box and lid black all over. The black paint will stop the light that enters through the hole from being reflected around inside the box.

3 Wearing gloves, plant a runner bean in a small pot of soil mix. Water the soil each day to keep it moist, but not too wet. On some days, no water may be needed.

4 When the plant has a shoot, stand it at the bottom of your maze. Close the lid and place the maze in a sunny spot. Once a day, remove the lid to see if the seedling needs watering.

The plant will find its way through the maze as it steadily moves toward the light. Eventually, it will poke out through the hole at the top of the shoe box.

Natural water pumps

When you look at a tree, you only see a part of it. Unseen roots spread out underground as wide as the branches above. These roots anchor a tree in the ground and hold it up against the force of the wind. Roots also help the tree to grow, by taking up water and nutrients from the soil through the trunk to the leaves. Trees act like a natural pump – many trees over 50m/165ft tall pump hundreds of litres/gallons of water a day in order to grow. You can suck a drink up through a straw, but trees cannot do this. They use a method called osmosis to draw the water upwards. The first experiment shows how osmosis works. Water inside the roots (sap) has a higher concentration of sugar than the water outside. The process of osmosis draws water from the soil, where the concentration is low, to inside the root, where concentration is high.

The second experiment uses dyed water to show how water actually travels up a plant's root. All living things are made up of little units called cells. Water can travel through cell walls but sugars cannot. During osmosis, water always moves in a set direction – from the side where there is less sugar dissolved in it to the side where there is more.

▲ Suck it and see
To find out how difficult it is to suck up water, carefully tape together straws with adhesive tape. The longer the straw, the more difficult it is for you to suck up the drink. The best mechanical pumps can only manage 10m/30ft.

How osmosis works

YOU WILL NEED

large potato, ruler, chopping board, peeler, knife, teaspoon, two shallow dishes, water, sugar.

1 You will need a large, smooth potato about 10cm/4in long and 6cm/2½in across. Carefully peel the potato on a chopping board to protect the work surface.

2 Cut the peeled potato in half, and then slice off the rounded ends. You will now have two round potato slices. Each slice should be about 3cm/1½in thick.

3 Use a teaspoon to scoop out a hollow in each potato slice. Place each slice in its own shallow dish and fill the dishes with water to about 1cm/ 1½in in depth.

4 Half fill both hollows with water. Add 2.5ml/½ tsp of sugar to one hollow. Cover and leave the potatoes for one day. (*Dye has been added to the water here to make it show up.*)

5 The level of liquid in the sugary hollow has risen. Osmosis has made more water move into this potato from the dish. The level in the other potato has not risen.

Osmosis in action

1 Pour some water into two tall drinking glasses. Add a few drops of ink or food dye to one of the glasses to give the water a strong, bright hue.

2 Use scissors to split the stem of the carnation lengthwise to about half way up the stem. Bind the stem with adhesive tape, so that it does not split any further.

Dyed water is drawn up one side of the split stem. The petals on that side of the flower have turned pink.

3 Place the glasses side by side on a window sill, and stand one half of the stem in each glass. Lean the flower against the window if it will not stand up on its own.

4 After a few hours, check to see what has happened. One half of the flower will be tinted with the dye. The other half of the flower will have remained white.

Seeds and plant life

Most plants reproduce by making seeds, which sprout and grow into new plants. To produce seeds, plants must be fertilized by pollen, usually from another plant of the same species (kind). Many plants rely on insects, such as bees and butterflies, to spread pollen. Seeds are mostly spread by animals that eat the fruit produced by plants, and by the wind. In some plants, such as those in rainforests, seeds may also be carried by water. The plants in your local area disperse (spread) their seeds in these ways, too. In the company of an adult, you can survey the seeds and plants in the local woods.

Performing a plant survey

1 Choose a patch of ground to sample and put in a peg. Measure 1m/1yd with the ruler, and put in another peg. Stretch and tie a piece of string between the pegs.

2 Now measure the remaining sides, pushing in two more pegs and stretching and tying string between them to mark out one square yard.

3 Measure and mark the midpoint of each piece of stretched string with pegs. Stretch more string between these pegs to divide the square into quarters.

4 Use your field guide to help you to identify the plant species growing in each quarter of the square. Do different plants, or the same ones, grow in each area?

5 Draw a chart on graph paper to record each plant's position. Use different colours for each plant type that you found. Add up the total number of each type of plant.

Looking at seed dispersal

1 Look for nibbled nuts and acorns. These seeds provide food for many animals. Collect seeds in a pot, cover them with fabric and secure with a rubber band.

2 Visit your local pond or stream to find seeds, such as alders, that are dispersed by water. Use your field guide to identify any seeds you see floating on the water.

3 Maple and sycamore trees have light seeds with wings. As they fall, the wings spin the seed through the air, helping it to fly farther and germinate far from the parent tree.

4 Find a dandelion head. Plants such as dandelions have very light seeds, each with its own small parachute of fine threads. These are carried away by the wind.

5 Look for the seed capsules of poppies. They are like pepper shakers with hundreds of tiny seeds inside. As the wind shakes the capsule, the seeds pop out and scatter widely.

When you walk through long grass, you may find burrs – fruits with tiny hooks – stuck on to your coat or to a pet's fur. Draw pictures of all the seeds and fruits that you find. Colour and label them.

Growing from fruit

There are many kinds of fruits grown in the garden. Some fruits are soft, such as apples and oranges, and others are hard, such as acorns and walnuts. Even tough little hawthorn berries and sycamore wings are fruits. Fruits all have seeds protected inside a container. The container may be the soft flesh of a plum or the hard shell of a hazelnut. You can discover the seeds inside different fruits. Some examples are given here. If you want to try others, use fruits bought from your local grocery store since some wild berries are poisonous.

orange   apple

plum

lemon

apricot

◀ **Soft fruits**

These fruits are soft, fleshy, and sweet. Like most fruits, they have grown from the reproductive ovaries inside female flowers. Open any fruit, and inside you will find seeds.

Looking at apple seeds

1 Cut open an apple with a sharp knife. Inside you will find several brown seeds in the middle. Use the tweezers to remove as many of the seeds as you want.

2 Use the tweezers to carefully remove the soft outer skin of a seed. Underneath the skin, you will find the slippery white seed. Treat it carefully – it is very delicate.

3 Look under a magnifier to see the embryo (at the tip). The rest of the seed is the cotyledon, which provides food so the embryo will grow into a new root and shoot.

Looking inside a nut

1 Nuts are fruits that have their seeds inside a hard shell. Carefully crack open a hazelnut with a pair of nutcrackers, and look for the nut kernel (seed) inside.

2 Use scissors to scrape off the dark outer skin from the kernel. You should then be able to separate the white hazelnut into two halves. Look at these with a magnifying glass.

3 Inside the nut is a tiny embryo. This part grows into roots and a stem. The two larger parts are the cotyledons, which supply energy for the sprouting seed to grow.

How a seed grows

1 Curl blotting paper inside a jar. Push a bean seed halfway down between the paper and the glass. Add water to a depth of 2cm/¾in and stand the jar in a light, warm place.

2 When the seed germinates, you will see the root growing downwards. Turn the jar so that the root points to the right. What do you think will happen?

As the root continues to grow, it changes direction so that it is growing downwards again.

Tropical seeds

1 An avocado pit is the seed of the avocado plant. Clean off any flesh left on the pit, and then carefully push three toothpicks into the pit, as shown above.

2 Fill a glass jar with water and suspend the pit, so that it just touches the waterline. Keep the jar in a warm, shady place, and top up the water regularly.

3 When roots begin to grow downwards, plant the pit in a pot filled with soil mix. Place the pot where the air is warm and humid, and wait for your seedling to grow.

Life in the forest

People who live in forests build their homes from materials found in the forest. In South America, the Yanomami tribe's large, round huts are made with trees bent into a dome shape, lashed with vines and thatched with palm leaves. The Yanomami sleep on the roof in hammocks made of woven grasses, slung from the rafters. Scientists who work in rainforests sometimes build temporary shelters with branches. You can build a shelter by following these instructions, but you may need the help of an adult. When looking for branches to make your shelter with, take an adult with you. Collect the branches from your backyard or a public area. Do not cut them from trees – always gather them from the ground, where they have fallen naturally.

YOU WILL NEED

five sturdy branches, rope or thick string, a friend or adult to help, ropes or strings, eight pegs, tarpaulin, ground sheet, two poles.

▲ Temperate forests

Beech, ash and oak grow in this northern European forest. Birds and squirrels live in the trees. Bluebells and wood anemones grow on the forest floor. Worms, moles and badgers burrow underground. Larger animals include deer, wild pigs and bears.

▲ Conifer forests

Hemlocks, cypresses and giant redwoods grow in conifer forests in North America. Woodpeckers and chipmunks search for food in the trees. Ferns grow on the forest floor. Moose and beavers live near lakes, and black bears scavenge for food.

▲ Trees in the savanna

The African savanna is dotted with drought-resistant trees, such as baobabs (bottle trees) and acacias. Herds of zebra, antelope and gazelles feed on grass. Taller giraffes and elephants can reach up into the trees for fresh leaves.

▲ Tropical rainforest

Many trees and climbing plants live in tropical rainforests, such as the Amazon of South America. Monkeys and bright birds live high up in the trees, where there is light and food. Dense, rotting vegetation covers the ground.

Build a shelter

1 Lash the ends of two sturdy branches together with rope or string. Stand the branches upright to make an A-frame. You could tie the A-frame to a tree for extra support.

2 Lash two more branches together. Stand them upright about 2m/6¼ft from the first A-frame. Place a lighter branch on top to make a ridge pole and lash it in place.

3 Attach two ropes or strings to each of the A-frames and peg the ropes securely into the ground. Now throw a tarpaulin over the ridge pole to form the roof.

4 Attach some ropes or strings to the eyeholes in the corners of the tarpaulin, and peg them securely into the ground. Stretch the tarpaulin tight to make the roof.

5 Thread string through the eyeholes on opposite sides of the ground sheet, to make the sheet into a sort of tube. Push two poles inside the sheet, one on each side.

6 Pull the two poles apart to make a stretcher shape that will fit inside the shelter. This will form the hammock, so that you will be able to rest off the ground.

7 Wedge the stretcher inside your shelter, so that the poles rest on the outside of the upright A-frames. Make sure your hammock is secure and will not slip down the poles.

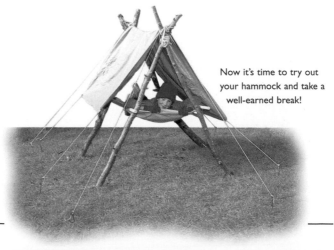

Now it's time to try out your hammock and take a well-earned break!

Soil erosion

All around the world, rainforests are being cut down at an alarming rate. At the beginning of the 1900s, tropical forests covered about twice the area they do today. Experts estimate that an area of rainforest about the size of England is lost each year. One of the main reasons for this is logging – the felling of trees for timber. Many rainforest trees are made of valuable hardwoods, such as teak and mahogany, which are used for building houses and making furniture. Trees are also cleared to create roads and new pasture for cattle.

The roots of trees and other plants help to hold forest soil together. When the trees are felled, the soil is left bare. During heavy rainfall, the earth is washed away, just as it is in the first project. However, when forests are left alone, they sustain themselves indefinitely, recycling water and nutrients from the soil. You can see how this works by growing a mini-jungle. The bottle or jar reproduces the warm, moist conditions and constant high temperatures of a rainforest. The plants recycle their own moisture, so they rarely need watering.

▲ **Vanishing forests**
This illustration shows the effects of deforestation. Tree roots help to hold the soil in place, and leaves absorb the force of falling rain. When forests are cut down, soil is washed away, and exposed earth dries up and hardens.

YOU WILL NEED
house plant, two plastic cups,
plant pot, soil or soil mix, two
watering cans.

Looking at soil erosion

1 Fit the house plant into the neck of one of the plastic cups. Fill the empty plant pot with soil or soil mix. Place the pot into the neck of the other plastic cup.

2 Pour water on to the house plant and into the pot of soil. What happens? You will find that water passes more quickly through the pot without the plant.

Water passing through the pot without the plant is muddy, because more soil has been washed through. Water passes more slowly through the pot with the plant. It will trickle through almost clear.

Plant a mini-jungle

YOU WILL NEED

large plastic bottle or jar with a lid,
gloves, gravel, charcoal, soil mix,
spoon or trowel, small tropical
plants, plant sprayer or watering can
with sprinkler rose.

1 Wash your large plastic bottle or jar to make sure that it is clean. Place handfuls of gravel into the bottom of the bottle, to make the lowest layer of the mini-jungle.

2 Combine a little charcoal with the soil mix. Add a deep layer of the mixture on top of the gravel, and then smooth out the soil so that it is level.

3 Make some large holes for the plants in the soil with a spoon or trowel. Then gently lift the plants out of their pots and lower them into the holes you have made.

4 Tamp the soil down around the base of each plant. You can use a spoon or a trowel to do this, if you find it difficult to reach that far with your fingers.

5 Spray the plants and soil quite thoroughly with water from a plant sprayer, or using a watering can with a sprinkler attachment. This is your tropical rain!

6 Put the lid on the bottle or jar, and your mini-jungle is complete. The water you have sprayed is recycled inside the bottle or jar, so you will not need to water your jungle often. Moisture from the plants condenses on the sides of the bottle or jar. It will then drip down into the soil, to be reused.

The balance of life

Life on Earth is a vast jigsaw of plant and animal activity. The world can be split into vegetation regions according to the kind of plants that thrive there. Scientists often break down the vegetation regions into smaller units, such as tropical rainforests or freshwater lakes. They might go further to identify individual trees or a pond. Each unit, where the creatures living there interact with each other, is called an ecosystem.

An ecosystem is a community of living things, or organisms, that all depend on each other. An aquarium like the one in the project is a miniature freshwater ecosystem. All plants need particular conditions of soil and climate to survive. Animals also survive by adapting to, and interacting with, their surroundings and the local climate.

If a particular species from an ecosystem is removed, the existence of other living things is threatened. If the plants on which a certain caterpillar feeds are destroyed, the caterpillars die. Eventually, the birds that feed on the caterpillars, and the foxes that feed on the birds would starve.

▲ Building an ecosystem

When there is enough warmth and moisture in an area of bare, rocky land, simple plants grow. The first to take hold are mosses and lichens. They are followed by tough grasses, which hold the soil together. As they die and rot, they add nutrients to the soil, preparing it for bigger plants to grow. Soon there is enough to support small shrubs and tough trees, such as pines, and eventually deciduous trees such as oaks. This process is called vegetation succession. It would take about 200 years for deciduous woodland to evolve from the moss and lichen stage.

Feeding habits ▶

Humans and animals depend on other living things for food. This picture shows how this food chain or web works. A grasshopper eats a leaf of grass, a thrush may eat the grasshopper, and a kestrel may eat the thrush. When the kestrel dies, bacteria break its body down and add nutrients to the soil, so that new plants can grow. Herbivorous animals eat plants only. Carnivores are meat eaters, and omnivores eat both animals and plants. Plants make their own food from sunlight, and so they are called autotrophs (self-feeders).

Make your own aquarium ecosystem

1 Put the gravel in a net. Rinse it in a plastic bowl of water, or run it under the cold water tap in the sink. This will discourage the formation of green algae.

2 Spread the gravel unevenly over base of the tank to a depth of about 3cm/1¼in. Add rocks and pieces of wood. These give surfaces for snails to feed on.

3 Fill the tank to about the halfway mark with tap water. Pour the water gently from a jug to avoid disturbing the landscape and churning up the gravel.

4 Add some water plants from an aquarium store. Keep some of them in their pots, but remove the others gently. Then root them in the gravel.

5 Now add a pitcherful of pondwater. This will contain organisms, such as *daphnia* (water fleas), which add to the life of your aquarium. You can buy pondwater in a garden store.

6 Add a few of the water animals you have collected from local ponds, such as tadpoles in frog spawn, or water snails. Take care not to overcrowd the aquarium.

7 Place the tank in bright light, but not in direct sunlight. You can watch the plants in the tank grow. Keep the water clean by removing dead matter from the gravel every few weeks.

Animal tracks and footprints

Wild creatures in the forest usually run away when humans approach. However, you can learn a lot about birds and other animals by looking at their tracks. You could go to a wood with an adult to hunt for animal tracks on soft or wet ground. The banks of streams and rivers are often criss-crossed by prints from animals who have gone there to drink.

Different groups of animals (mammals, birds, reptiles and amphibians) leave different tracks. The first project shows you how to look for these prints. Tracks give clues about the size and weight of the animal. They also show how animals move – whether they run, hop, slide or slither. Large, heavy birds for example, such as geese, waddle along – shifting their weight from side to side. Their prints show that they place one foot in front of the other and slightly to the side, rather like the way humans walk. Small birds, such as sparrows and finches, hop along on thin legs and feet. They leave tracks of tiny prints running side by side. Draw the prints or take a photograph, and record in a notebook the date and place, ground conditions and other observations. The second project shows you how to make casts of the most interesting footprints.

▲ **Out and about**
Study the tracks that you have found very carefully. What do they tell you about the way the animal that made them moved – did it hop, run or waddle? Use a field guide to animal tracks to help you identify the animals that left them.

YOU WILL NEED

magnifying glass, camera, notebook, pencil, field guide.

Animal tracks

1 When you find a footprint, count the number of toes. Can you see any claws? A fox's paw is rounded, with four toes and claws. Take photos or make drawings of animal tracks you see.

2 Deer have narrow, split hooves with just two toes. They leave deep tracks, because they walk with all their weight on their toes, rather than evenly spread throughout their feet.

3 Most birds have long, spindly feet, with either three or four toes. All ducks and some wading birds have webbed feet. The web shows up in the outline of the print.

Footprint cast

YOU WILL NEED

protective gloves, field guide, thin card, paper clip, plaster of Paris, water, mixing bowl, spoon, trowel, scrubbing brush, paintbrush, paints or varnish, water pot.

1 Find a clear animal track, either in sand or dry mud. Remove any loose twigs or leaves around the print. (Remember to wear gloves if you are working in soil.)

2 Look for bird footprints in wet sand or mud. Tracks show the size of the bird that made it, and what group of birds it belongs to. Use a field guide to identify the bird that made the print.

3 Bend a strip of card into a ring large enough to fit around the print, and fasten the card ring with a paper clip. Place the ring over the print.

4 Mix the plaster of Paris with a little water in a bowl, according to the instructions on the packet. Stir the mixture until it is a thick and even paste with no lumps.

5 Carefully spoon enough plaster of Paris on to the print to cover it completely. After 15 minutes, the cast will be dry enough for you to pick it up.

6 Use a trowel to prize the cast loose. Carefully peel off the paper ring. Clean up the cast by brushing off any loose soil or sand with a scrubbing brush.

7 Allow the plaster cast to dry for 24 hours. After this, you could paint or varnish the cast. Try painting the raised footprint one colour and the background another colour.

Finished casts of dog and bird footprints.

Searching for insects

Insects make up three-quarters of all animal species (kinds) on the Earth. Insects are everywhere, so they are easy to find. The best place to start is your backyard or a local park. If there is a good range of plants, up to 300 species of beetles can be found in a very small area, such as gardens. There may be up to 200 kinds of flies, 90 different bugs and many species of bees, ants, wasps, moths and butterflies.

To identify the species living in a particular area, scientists mark a square, and search all the places where creatures hide – under leaves, stones and logs, and in tiny crevices in trees. Scientists may leave pitfall traps in the ground or hang traps in the trees. You can find creatures locally using the type of trap demonstrated in the first project. The second project shows you how to make a simple pooter, which enables you to collect insects without harming them. Wear gloves when handling insects, because some may sting or bite. Always take an adult out with you.

▲ Feet tasters

The housefly has taste sensors on its feet. It sucks up its liquid through spongy mouthparts as soon as it lands.

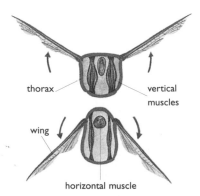

▲ How insects fly

Insects have no muscles in their wings. Instead the wings are hinged to the insect's thorax. They move up and down as the thorax changes shape. As the roof of the thorax is pulled down, the wings flick up. As the ends of the thorax are pulled in, the wings flick down.

Pitfall trap

1 If you have a backyard, ask an adult to show you a place where you can dig a small hole. Use a trowel to dig a hole in damp earth, which is large enough for the jar to fit in.

2 Place the jar in the hole. Firm the earth back around the sides of the jar with your hands. Put small, fresh leaves in the bottom of the jar for minibeast bait.

3 Place some small stones around the trap, and balance a large flat stone or tile on top, to prevent the minibeast trap from filling up with rain. Leave it overnight.

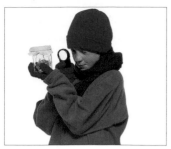

4 In the morning, remove the jar. Place a piece of thin white fabric over the top and secure it with a rubber band. Study any minibeasts you have caught using a magnifying glass.

5 Use a field guide to identify the minibeasts you have caught. When you have finished, remember to release the creatures near to where you found them.

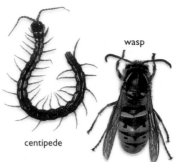

wasp

centipede

▲ Show a leg

Centipedes, like insects, are members of the arthropod group. They have many legs, one pair on each body segment. Adult insects, such as this queen wasp, have bodies in three main sections and six legs. Most also have wings.

Make a pooter

1 Cut off the bottom of the plastic bottle. Roll out one large and one small ball of modelling material. Flatten out the large ball and shape it over the bottom of the bottle.

2 To make a filter, cut a short piece of straw. Secure a piece of fabric around the straw with a rubber band. Push the other end through the small lump of modelling material.

3 Fit the filter into the neck of the bottle by shaping the modelling material. Make a hole in the bottom flap with a sharp pencil. Push a long straw into the hole you have made.

4 Look for a small insect to study. (Big insects would get damaged.) Aim the end of the long straw over the insect. Suck on the short straw to draw the insect safely into the pooter.

5 When you have finished studying your insect, take it back to where you found it. To release the insect, carefully remove the bottom flap and shake the insect out.

What is an insect?

YOU WILL NEED

Drawing insects: magnifying glass, pencil, notebook, coloured pencils.

Insect survey: gloves, four tent pegs, string, tape measure, glass jar, magnifying glass, pen, notebook, field guide, coloured pencils.

Birds, reptiles, and mammals all have internal skeletons to provide a framework for their bodies. Insects are different – they have skeletons on the outside. Their soft body parts are protected by a hard case called an exoskeleton. This forms a waterproof barrier around the insect. It prevents the insect from drying out and air from passing through. Unlike birds and mammals, insects are cold-blooded animals. This means the temperature of an insect's body is about the same as its surroundings. To warm up, an insect basks in the sunshine. When it gets too hot, it moves into the shade.

Insects are fragile. It can be difficult to pick them up and examine them without harming them. When studying insects, use a notebook to record what you see. Write down the date, time, weather conditions and place where you found the insect. Use a field guide to help you make an identification. The projects here show you how to keep a record of the insects that you see. Look at the mouthparts and antennae. Think about the shape of the insect's body. Is it short or long? Does the insect have hard wing cases, or long legs?

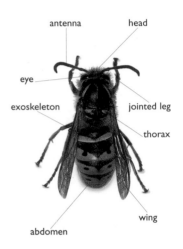

▲ **Wasp sections**
The bodies of adult insects have three sections – head, thorax and abdomen. Like this wasp, each section is made of small plates that fit together at flexible joints. The head carries the mouth parts, antennae and eyes. The legs and wings are attached to the thorax. The abdomen contains the reproductive organs and part of the digestive system.

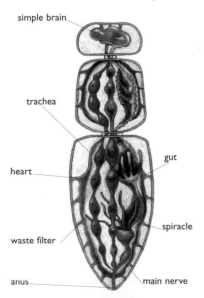

◄ **Inside the insect**
An insect's internal systems are protected by its hard exoskeleton. This diagram shows the main systems separated and tinted to make them clear. The nervous system (purple) sends messages from the senses to the brain. In the respiratory system (gray), air enters the body through tiny holes along each side of the insect's body, called spiracles. Pipes called tracheae carry the air to other parts of the body. In the circulatory system (red), several hearts, arranged in a row, pump blood around the body. The digestive system (green, orange) processes food.

Drawing insects

1 Find an insect and use the magnifying glass to study it closely. Start by drawing three ovals to show the head, the thorax and the abdomen of the insect.

2 Can you see the insect's legs? Copy them on your drawing. Now copy the size and shape of the insect's antennae. Draw the eyes and add the outline of the wings.

3 Now draw any markings that you notice on the insect's body and wings (if it has them). Finish your drawing by shading it in as accurately as you can.

Insect survey

1 Find an area of long grass. Wearing gloves to protect your hands, use the tent pegs, a measuring tape, and string to mark a square measuring 1m/1yd on each side.

2 What insects can you find inside the square? Use a collecting jar and a magnifying glass to study them. Write down what you have found in a notebook.

3 Now mark out a square yard in a different place. Try an area with flowers or a hedge. You may find aphids and greenfly on plant stems, and shieldbugs under leaves.

4 Move a fallen log to see what kinds of insects live underneath. Make sure you wear gloves to protect your hands. You may find beetles under logs, and woodlice and earwigs under bark.

5 Still wearing gloves, carefully look under some stones. What kinds of creatures prefer this dark, damp habitat? You may find worms, snails, ground beetles or an ants' nest.

Use your field guide to identify your discoveries. How many different species did you find in each area? Make a chart to record the results of your survey.

Studying insect life

Woods are great places to go insect watching. Trees offer food and shelter from the weather, so they are an ideal habitat for insects. The number of insects you find may depend on the season. In the spring, wild flowers bloom and attract insects. In the summer, the woods offer insects sunny clearings and cool shade. Choose a large tree and make a survey of all the insects you can find on a single branch. Make a tree trap to catch insects active at night.

Many insects depend on plants, but many plants depend on insects too. Insects help to pollinate plants by carrying pollen from the same plant to another of its species. Many plants have pink, red or orange flowers, because these are the tones that butterflies see well. Other flowers have special markings called nectar guides, leading from the base of the petals. Some show up only in ultraviolet light. Insects such as bees have eyes that are sensitive to this light, and they follow these guides to the middle of the flower.

▲ Insect pollination

This wasp is visiting a flower to feed on its sugary nectar. It sucks up the nectar with its tongue, to feed the larvae (young) in its nest. As the wasp reaches into the center of the flower, pollen from the flower rubs off on the insect's body. This is then carried by the wasp to the next flower.

Human vision

Insect vision

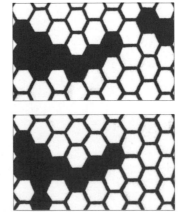

◀ Seeing is believing

Insect vision is very different from ours. Experts think each lens of an insect's compound eye sees a small part of a scene. This gives a mosaic-like view that is built up into a bigger picture. These diagrams compare how we see a moving insect, and what experts think an insect sees. An insect can sense tiny movements our eyes would hardly notice, because they have many more lenses that are affected.

Make a tree trap

1 Using a pair of sharp scissors, carefully cut the plastic bottle in half widthways. Ask an adult to help you to do this, if you find it too difficult.

2 Turn the neck half of the bottle around and push it inside the bottom half. Now tape the two halves of the bottle together using strong adhesive tape.

3 Cut a long piece of string. Loop the string around the open end of the trap and tie it into a knot. Place a small piece of ham inside the trap to act as insect bait.

4 Carefully tie the trap along the branch of a tree, or hang the trap down underneath the branch. Leave the trap out overnight. Go back the next morning to check it.

5 Use your field guide to identify the insects that you have caught. Record your findings in a notebook. Release the insects when you have identified them.

Life on a branch

1 Spread out the white sheet below a branch. Shake the branch to dislodge the insects on to the sheet. If the branch is high, tap it with a stick. Be sure not to damage the tree.

2 Sweep the insects that drop on to the sheet into collecting jars for you to study. Use a paintbrush to carefully transfer the insects without harming them.

Use a field guide to identify the insects. Try surveying another type of tree. Make a chart, as above, to show the different species found on the various trees.

Insects in disguise

Most insects try to escape from predators by flying away. But it is even better not to be seen at all. Insects that hunt other creatures also need to be invisible to creep up unnoticed on their prey. Many insects have special tones and patterns on their bodies to help them look like leaves, seeds, twigs or stones. These natural disguises are called camouflage.

Stick insects change their body tone to match their surroundings, and so remain hidden almost anywhere. Their long slender bodies and sticklike legs make them hard to see among twigs and leaves. Stick insects are easy to take care of at home. You can buy them at some pet stores. Try the test opposite to find out more about camouflage.

You could look outside for ways in which insects disguise themselves. The last project shows you how to attract insects, such as butterflies and wasps, by planting flowers and herbs. Remember to ask permission from an adult before you start.

▲ **Hidden hunter**
Insects are attracted by the bright colours and sweet scents of flowers. The markings on this wasp are almost the same as the flower it is feeding on.

▲ **Prickles and bristles**
A pair of giant, prickly leaf insects with the green female (*right*) and the smaller male (*left*). The wings of the male are folded along its back. The safest way to pick up leaf or stick insects is by placing your fingers on each side of the body.

YOU WILL NEED

Camouflage test: scissors, light and dark green paper, two cardboard boxes, tape, stick insects, paintbrush, privet or ivy leaves, kitchen paper, white fabric, non-hardening modelling material, notebook, coloured pencils.

Rearing stick insects: earth, small tank or large jar, privet or ivy leaves, glass of water, sticks, stick insects, kitchen paper.

Plant a window box: garden gloves, window box or large tub, earth, soil mix (optional), packet of wildflower seeds, watering can, notebook, pencil, field guide.

Camouflage test

1 Cut pieces of paper to line the insides of the cardboard boxes. Make one box light green, and the other dark green. Attach the paper with adhesive tape.

2 Transfer your stick insects with a paintbrush to the light green box. Add leaves and damp kitchen paper. Cover with white fabric weighted at the corners with modelling material.

3 Leave the box in a light place for a day. Record the insects' colour with coloured pencils. Put the insects in the darker box. After a day, check to see if they have changed.

Rearing stick insects

1 Put a layer of earth in the bottom of a tank or a large jar, with a tight-fitting lid with small air holes. Add privet or ivy leaves in a glass of water, some sticks and your stick insects.

2 Put some wet kitchen paper in a corner, so that the insects have enough moisture. Remember to replace the paper regularly. Ask the pet store if your insects need anything else.

Plant a window box

1 Wearing gloves, fill a window box or a large tub with earth. You could add some soil mix to the earth, and mix it in. The container should be about three-quarters full of earth.

2 Scatter wildflower seeds over the soil. You can buy seeds, such as daisy and bird's-foot trefoil, at a nursery. Do not dig up wild plants. Cover the seeds with more earth.

3 The seedlings will come up in a few weeks. Water the young plants regularly. As the plants grow, record in your notebook which insects visit and feed on them.

Insects to watch

As insects eat, they leave behind damaged plants and other signs of feeding. Sometimes these signs are easier to spot than the insects themselves. Look in a small area, such as a fallen log, a shrub, or a bush. Hundreds of insects will be near, but most are small and wary. Discover the eating habits and preferences of different insects in the first project.

Look for freshwater insects, such as beetles and bugs in ponds and streams. Spring and summer are good times to look, because the young insects turn into adults at these times. You could even make a small pool for insects in your yard. Ask a responsible adult if you may dig the pond. To catch water insects, you will need a net, which you can make easily yourself. When you catch insects at the pond, take an adult with you for safety. Approach the water quietly, to disturb the wildlife as little as possible. Different insects live in various places in the pond or stream. Some live near the surface, while others swim near the bottom. Gently lift up stones and pebbles to find the creatures that lurk on the underside. Always replace them carefully, so that you disturb the habitat as little as possible.

▲ **Mmm, tasty...**
Most plant-eating insects prefer one particular food, and may eat only a part of that food plant. Some insects leave ragged holes in leaves. Aphids and other bugs leave brown and yellow lines on crops when they suck out the sap.

Food samples

YOU WILL NEED

cardboard, pair of compasses and a pencil, scissors, four garden sticks, small samples of food (such as honey, meat, cheese and fruit), notebook, field guide.

1 Draw four circles on the cardboard with the compasses. Cut them out. Use the point of a pencil to make holes in the middles of the circles. Push the sticks through the holes.

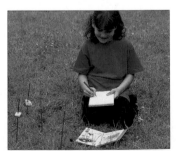

2 Plant the sticks in the ground. Push the food samples on the sticks, so they rest on the circles. Do insects prefer certain foods? Are there more insects around at different times of day?

Insect pool

1 Wear gloves when you are making your insect pool. Dig a hollow in the ground with the trowel. The hole should be big enough to fit an old plastic bowl inside.

2 Place the bowl in the hollow and press it down firmly. Spread gravel on the bottom and put in the water plants. Place stones arond the edge of the bowl and inside it.

3 Then fill the bowl with water, using a watering can. Your pool is now finished and ready for occupation. Insects and other animal life will soon be attracted to the pool.

Make a pond net

YOU WILL NEED

Insect pool: garden gloves, trowel, plastic bowl, gravel, water plants, large stones, watering can.

Make a pond net: wire, thin sock, pliers, long pole or broom handle, jubilee clip from a hardware store, screwdriver, jug (pitcher), empty plastic ice-cream container, magnifying glass, field guide.

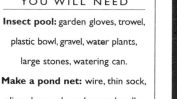

1 Begin your pond net by threading wire in and out through the top of a thin sock. You may need to use a pair of pliers to bend the wire into a circle.

2 Use the pair of pliers to twist the ends of the wire together, to make the net secure. Ask an adult to help if you need to. Now position the net at the end of a long pole.

3 Carefully thread the jubilee clip over the pole, and push the twisted wires under the clip, as shown above. Tighten the clip using a screwdriver. Ask an adult to help you do this.

4 Down at the pond, capture insects by sweeping your net gently through the water. Lightly tap the stems of plants to knock other insects into your net.

5 Empty a jug of pond water into a container. Empty your net into it. Study the creatures you have caught. Tip the water and creatures back into the pond when you have finished.

Moths and butterflies

All butterflies and moths go through a metamorphosis (change). They start as caterpillars then, as pupae, encase themselves in a cocoon, where a remarkable change takes place, and they finally emerge as adults. Caterpillars feed on leafy plants, such as grasses and nettles. Adult moths and butterflies gather on plants with nectar-bearing flowers. As you will see from the projects here, bright lights and a mixture of fruit and sugar will bring moths fluttering.

Some butterflies have wings with warning markings. The markings tell predators that they are poisonous to eat. Other butterflies are harmless, but mimic (copy) poisonous species. Their markings fool predators into avoiding them, too. The best way to attract butterflies is to plant a butterfly garden. Choose plants that bloom at various times of the year.

▲ Beating around the bush
The sweet-smelling purple buddleia is a popular plant with butterflies, and so has gained the nickname butterfly bush. Butterflies attracted to buddleia include small tortoiseshells (*shown here*), peacocks, painted ladies, commas and red admirals.

▲ Antennae ID
You can tell a butterfly from a moth by looking at the antennae (feelers). Many butterflies have antennae with clubbed tips, like this swallowtail. Moths' antennae vary, but most are straight or feathered.

Torchlight attraction

1 Wearing gloves, dig a small hole in the garden with a trowel. Do this in the daylight, and remember to ask an adult's permission first before you start to dig.

2 Check that your torch fits inside the hole. At dusk turn on the torch and put it inside the hole. Fill any gaps with earth to hold the torch securely in position.

3 Step back and watch the moths flutter around the light. You could try taking flash photographs of the insects with a camera. How did your photos turn out?

Sweet moth feast

1 Begin by measuring out about 500g/1¼lb/scant 2 cups of soft light brown sugar with a spoon into your scales, or a measuring bowl. Pour the measured sugar into your mixing bowl.

2 Add the overripe fruit to the mixing bowl, and mash it with a fork. Keep mashing until the fruit has become a pulp. Add some warm water until the mixture becomes runny.

3 Paint the mixture on to a tree trunk or a fence post. Return when it is dark. Take a torch to help you see the moths feeding, and a field guide to help you to identify them.

Butterfly garden

YOU WILL NEED

Torchlight attraction: garden gloves, trowel, torch (flashlight), camera.
Sweet moth feast: soft light brown sugar, spoon, food scales, mixing bowl, ripe fruit, fork, warm water, paintbrush, torch (flashlight), field guide.
Butterfly garden: seeds or young plants, gloves, trowel, rake, watering can, notebook, pencil, field guide.

1 First you need to grow some plants from seed – or buy young plants. Wearing a pair of gloves, dig up your chosen patch of earth with a trowel.

2 Break up any large clods of earth with a rake or trowel. Now start to rake over the top of your plot, so that the earth is evenly spread and crumbly.

3 Dig several small holes for your plants with the trowel. Place the plants in the holes, and press the earth down firmly with gloved hands around the base of each plant.

4 Water the plants well. They will need to be watered regularly through the spring and summer. The sun will scorch wet leaves during the day, so water your plants at dusk.

5 Record which butterflies you see visiting your flowers. A field guide will help you to identify them. Which species prefer which flowers? And which is the most popular plant?

Watching a caterpillar grow

These projects show you how to prepare a home for caterpillars. Look for caterpillars on plants where you see half-eaten leaves – they may be hiding on the undersides. Take some of these leaves with the caterpillars you find. Use a field guide to identify the species you have found, and which plants they prefer. Try not to touch caterpillars directly with your fingers, since some species may sting. Pick them up with a paintbrush, or encourage them to climb on to a leaf. Carry them in a jar. At home, keep the caterpillars out of direct sunlight, in a moist, cool place. Try not to disturb them. Clean the box regularly, and replace old leaves with fresh ones.

> ### YOU WILL NEED
> scissors, cardboard box, adhesive tape, thin white fabric or netting, non-hardening modelling material, rubber gloves, fresh leaves, kitchen paper, collecting jar containing caterpillars, ruler, pencil, notebook, field guide, coloured pencils.

◄ Complete metamorphosis

When butterflies, moths, ants and bees change during their lives, it is called complete metamorphosis. The life cycle of the elephant hawk moth (shown here) has four separate stages. The moth begins life as an egg. The egg hatches a caterpillar, which spends almost all of its time feeding. When the caterpillar is fully grown, it burrows into the ground and sheds its skin to reveal a pupa, a stage at which the larva changes into the adult insect when cocooned in a protective case. Finally, the case splits and the adult moth emerges.

Keeping caterpillars

1 Cut holes in the sides of the box for windows. Using strong tape, cut out and stick pieces of fabric or netting over the windows to cover them securely.

2 Now cut a large piece of thin white fabric to make the cage lid. Weight the corners of the fabric down with modelling material, to prevent the caterpillars from escaping.

3 Wearing a pair of gloves, put some fresh leaves inside the box. Make sure that they are from a plant your caterpillars eat. Be sure to provide fresh leaves daily.

4 Put some damp kitchen paper in a corner of the box to provide moisture. Carefully transfer your caterpillars from the collecting jar to the box. Cover with the lid.

5 Check your caterpillars every day, and replace the damp kitchen paper. Record how much they eat and how big they are. Remember to replace the leaves daily.

6 Watch how your caterpillars feed and move around on the leaves. Record the dates when you see them moulting (shedding skin). How many times did they shed their skins?

7 When it has finished growing, the caterpillar will change into a pupa, or chrysalis. It will attach itself to the stem of a food plant, and form a new skin. Make a note of the date.

8 Check your pupa every day, and write down the date when you see the case splitting. Compare your two dates. How long did the insect spend as a pupa?

9 You will see a butterfly or moth struggle out of the old skin. The insect rests and pumps blood into its crumpled wings to straighten them out before flying off.

June–July	caterpillar feeds	
end July		pupa forms
mid-August		butterfly emerges

Keep a chart of the life cycles of your insects.

When the caterpillars become adult moths or butterflies, it is time to let them go. Take the insects back to where you found them. Lift the lid off the box, and let them fly away.

Crawling colonies

Unlike most insects, ants live in colonies. They are known as social insects, as opposed to solitary insects. Ants are different to flying insects, such as butterflies and bees, yet they behave in a similar way. An ant colony is like an underground city with millions of insects, each with its own role to play. Queen ants (of which there may be several in one nest) lay eggs. Undeveloped females called workers perform the essential tasks of the colony. They scurry around, searching for food, and bring it to the nest.

eggs   queen's chamber   waste

pupae

workers   young ants hatch   worker and larvae

The key to the smooth running of the colony is good communication. Ants cannot see well, so they communicate by touch and smell. When two ants meet, they touch antennae (feelers). When an ant finds a food source, it hurries back to the nest, pressing its body close to the ground as it runs. This leaves a trail of scent, which the other ants can follow to reach the food.

▲ Inside an ants' nest

Ants' nests are usually underground. A nest has many chambers, or rooms, and passages. Different chambers contain the eggs, larvae (young), pupae and the queen. Other chambers are used to store food and waste. Worker ants alter the temperature of the nest by opening or closing passages.

> YOU WILL NEED
>
> garden gloves, peeled ripe fruit,
>
> piece of paper, magnifying glass.

Watching ant trails

1 Wearing gloves, find a trail of ants. Follow the trail to discover where the ants are going. Does the trail lead to food? Rub out part of the trail and see what happens.

2 Now put fruit down on a piece of paper near the trail of ants. The paper will make it easier to see the ants. When the workers find the fruit, watch and see what happens.

3 Once an ant has laid a scent trail to the fruit, others will follow. Move the fruit to another part of the paper. What happens next? Do the ants go straight to the new food site?

Make an ant home

1 Measure and carefully cut a piece
of purple paper that is large
enough to fit around the jar. Secure
the paper in position around the jar
with tape.

2 Wearing a pair of gloves, use
the trowel to fill the jar with
earth until the jar is almost full.
Carefully place a few leaves on top
of the earth.

3 Capture some garden ants using a
paintbrush and collecting jar. Let
the ants crawl on to the paintbrush.
Then tap the jar, so that the ants fall in.
Transfer the ants to their new home.

4 Feed your ants with a piece of ripe
fruit or some preserve. Some damp
kitchen paper will provide moisture.
Feed your ants daily and refresh the
leaves and moist paper regularly.

5 Cover the top of the jar with
a piece of thin white fabric, so that
the ants cannot escape. Secure the
fabric with adhesive tape. Keep your
ant home in a cool place.

6 After a few days, remove the tape
and lift the paper to observe your
ant home. There will now be winding
tunnels, built by the ants, against the
sides of the jar.

If you have caught a queen ant, you
may see the workers tending the eggs
or larvae in special chambers.

Feed the birds

Put bird food out in a safe place, and you will discover one of the best ways of studying birds close up. You can make your own bird cake, such as the one here, and put out kitchen scraps such as stale breadcrumbs, cheese, fruit, cooked rice, cooked pasta, uncooked pastry and bacon rind. Birds will really appreciate these tidbits, particularly in cold weather, when the ground is hard to peck at for worms and trees are bare of fruit and berries. Count how many different kinds of birds visit. Also, notice which species (kind) prefer each kind of food. Note down the date, time and weather when you first see a new species. Do the birds feed quietly together, or do they fight over the scraps?

▲ Winter feed
Fruit is an important food for many birds, particularly in winter. Garden species, such as thrushes and blackbirds will peck at apples, leaving large, irregular holes.

◄ Shells and nuts
Look for nut shells gnawed by animals. Squirrels and mice leave neat holes and teethmarks. Birds leave peckmarks or jagged edges, or they crack nuts in half, such as the top two nuts here. Song thrushes feed on snails. They smash the shell against a stone. The stone is called the thrush's anvil. You may be lucky and find shell remains beside a stone.

Make a bird cake

1 Soften the vegetable fat on a radiator or get an adult to help you melt it in a pan. Chop the nuts, then mix with the oatmeal and crumbs in a bowl. Add the melted fat and mix.

2 Cut a long piece of string. Tie a really big knot in one end. Put the string into the cup, so that the knotted end is at the bottom, and spoon the mixture into the cup.

3 Ensure that the end of the string comes out through the middle of the mixture. When the mixture is set, pull the string to remove the cake. Hang it on a tree branch or window sill.

Build a bird table

1 Lay the wooden strips along the edges of your plywood board, as shown. Now glue the strips of wood into position, so that the ends fit neatly together.

2 When the glue is dry, turn the board over. Carefully hammer nails through it, into the strips. If you find using a hammer difficult, you could ask an adult to help you to do this.

3 Paint the top surface of your bird table with a coat of varnish, to make it waterproof. When this coat is dry, turn the table over, and coat the underside too.

4 Screw eye-hooks into the strips at the four corners of the table. Now cut two pieces of string about 30cm/12in long. Tie the ends of the strings to the hooks.

Your bird table is now ready to be positioned. Hang it from a tree by easing the strings over a strong branch. Adjust the strings, until the table hangs down evenly.

Telltale bird traces

In nature, birds peck at nuts, fruit and berries. Their beaks leave telltale marks. These signs can help you to identify the birds that made them. A good field guide will help you to find out whether food remains have been left by birds rather than small animals, such as mice and squirrels. Hunters, such as owls, leave special food remains behind. They swallow voles, mice and even small birds whole. Once or twice a day, the bird chokes up the remains that it cannot digest, in a tightly packed ball, or pellets. By examining a pellet closely, as in the second project, you can discover exactly what the hunting animal caught the previous day.

Bird feathers are made of a flexible substance, called keratin, that is also found in human hair and nails. They are amazingly strong, but weigh almost nothing. Feathers are windproof and most are waterproof. Feathers are used in flying and to help keep birds warm and dry. Some male birds use bright plumage (feathers) to attract a mate. The shade of plumage may also help to camouflage a bird from predators. Watch for dropped feathers around your bird table.

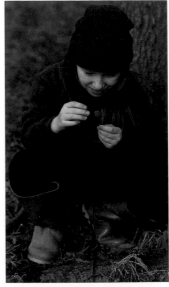

▲ Searching for pellets
Look around the base of trees for all kinds of interesting animal remains. Pellets left by hunting birds are found under trees with low branches, where the birds may perch.

▼ Mounting feathers
Cut slits in a page of a notebook and slide them in. This also makes the feathers easy to remove.

▲ Light as air
Down feathers are light and fluffy. They lie next to the bird's skin, and help keep the bird warm.

▲ Flying high
Flight feathers are found on the wings and tail, and are strong and stiff. Tail feathers help with steering.

◀ Flight aid
Body or contour feathers cover the bird's body and give it a streamlined shape, which helps it fly well.

Finding out about feathers

1 Study a bird's flight feather under a magnifying glass. Split the feather's barbs (individual strands). You can now observe the barbules (the fringed edges).

2 Repair the feather's surface, just as a bird does during preening. Smooth the barbs between your finger and thumb, so that they join back together properly.

3 Now try another experiment. Add a little water to some paint, and brush it on your flight feather. What happens to the paint? Why do you think this is?

Dissect an owl pellet

YOU WILL NEED

Finding out about feathers:

feathers, magnifying glass, water, paint, water pot, paintbrush.

Dissect an owl pellet: rubber gloves, owl pellet, bowl, warm water, dishwashing detergent, tweezers, kitchen paper, small box, tissue paper.

1 Wear rubber gloves for this project. First, soak the owl pellet in a bowl of warm water with a little dishwashing detergent added. Leave the pellet until it has softened.

2 Using a pair of tweezers, gently begin to pull the pellet apart. Inside, you will find the fur, teeth, skulls and other bones of small animals that the owl has eaten.

3 Use the tweezers to carefully separate the bones from the fur. Wash the bones in warm, soapy water, and pat them dry gently with a kitchen paper.

Line a small box with tissue paper. Choose a bright shade that will make the bones show up. Now arrange your bones. Can you identify the animal remains that you have found? There may be remains of voles, including skulls, jawbones and leg bones. It can also contain small stones that the owl had swallowed to help with digestion.

125

Bird travel and flight

Many birds travel vast distances each year. They may travel to escape the chill of winter, to find food or a safe nesting site. Departure is often triggered by the shortening daylight hours of the autumn. In the spring, the birds travel back again. These journeys are called migrations. Many species (kinds) do not feed while they travel, so must fatten up before they leave. Migrating birds face many dangers. They may get lost in storms or be killed by predators. Thousands die of hunger, thirst and exhaustion.

Flying takes up a lot of energy, but has many advantages for birds. Hovering uses the most energy of all. However, birds are able to save their energy by gliding on air currents. Large birds soar upwards into air currents, with their wings outstretched to trap as much air as possible. Making an aerofoil (airfoil) in the project opposite shows how the shape of a wing produces lift. Then build a spiral model to see how birds circle in warm air currents without flapping their wings.

▲ Lift and flight

A bird's wing is slightly curved at the top, and flatter underneath. A shape like this, which is designed to provide uplift in flight, is called an aerofoil (airfoil). As the bird moves through the air, the curved shape makes the air travel faster over the wing than beneath it. This makes an area of low air pressure above the wing, which allows the bird to rise. Aircraft are able to fly, because their wings are a similar shape to a bird's wings.

Migration routes

● White storks travel from Europe to South Africa via Gibraltar or the Middle East.

● Short-tailed shearwaters fly the length of the Pacific ocean, from Alaska to the Tasman Sea.

● Arctic tern

● Peregrine falcons migrate from Canada to Argentina. They are also found in Europe and Asia.

● American golden plover

● Swallows migrate from northern Europe and Asia, to South Africa and back again – nearly 20,000km/12,500 miles.

How a wing works

1 Cut a strip of paper about 30cm/ 12in long. Glue the ends together firmly. When the glue is dry, bend the paper into a wing shape, curved on top and flat underneath.

2 Mark the middle of the wing. Thread a long piece of thread on to a needle and push it through the middle of the wing. Gently pull the aerofoil (airfoil) down the thread.

3 Now get a friend to hold the thread taut. Blow hard against the curved edge of the aerofoil (airfoil), and watch the wing rise up the thread – just as an airplane or a bird's wing lifts.

Soaring spiral

1 Use a pair of compasses and a pencil to draw a circle on a piece of paper. Now draw and shade in a spiral shape with buzzards (or other birds) flying around it.

2 Carefully cut out the decorated paper spiral. Use a pencil to make the hole left in the middle of the spiral by your compasses, big enough to fit over the thimble.

3 Fit the pencil point into the reel. Put the pin in the eraser. Push the thimble through the hole in the paper spiral, so that it sits over the thimble. Balance the thimble on the pin.

4 Stand your model on a radiator. Now watch the buzzards circling around in the warm air currents that rise from the radiator. Your model must be well balanced to work properly.

Physical and Material Marvels

We live in a world of engineering marvels – of soaring sky scrapers, wide-spanning bridges, and massive dams. We can communicate with almost everyone, anywhere on the Earth, and even in Space. This section shows the part that science and technology have played in setting the pace of change. Science accumulates knowledge about the world by observation, study and experiment. Technology puts the knowledge into practical use as inventions, to improve the quality of life.

Chemical change

Over the past 100 years, scientists have invented many substances, such as plastics, medicines and detergents, that we take for granted today. These substances are created by chemical reactions. In a chemical reaction, a new substance (called a product) is made as a result of other substances (called reactants) undergoing chemical change. Many chemical reactions happen naturally, such as oil (petrol) and gas, which form from the remains of animals and plants. They are called hydrocarbons, because they are mixtures of hydrogen and carbon.

The following experiments demonstrate the three main ways in which chemical reactions can happen – by passing electricity through substances, by heating them, or simply by mixing them together. In the first, electricity breaks down salty water to make chlorine (the disinfectant often used in swimming pools). In the second, heat turns sugar, which is made from carbon, hydrogen and oxygen, into pure carbon. Finally, you make the gas used in some fire extinguishers by mixing bicarbonate of soda (baking soda) and vinegar together.

▲ **Checking up**
A technician is ensuring all the bottles of chemicals are correctly labelled. Accuracy is very important in science.

YOU WILL NEED
Electrolysis: battery (4–6 volts), bulb and holder, wires, wire strippers, screwdriver, paper clips, salt, jar, water.
Heat changes: old pan, teaspoon, sugar, stove.
Getting a reaction: teaspoon, bicarbonate of soda (baking soda), glass bowl, vinegar, matches.

WARNING!
Please take care when using electrical equipment. Always have an adult present.

How oil is formed

The story of oil begins in warm seas full of living things. As they die, they fall to the bottom of the sea floor to decay into thick, black mud.

In time, mud is buried beneath many layers of sand, with clay in between. The sediments (deposits) sink deeper and deeper, and also become hotter.

After millions of years, the sediments fold under pressure. Oil from the black mud is forced into sandstones and trapped under the layers of clay.

Electrolysis

1 With adult help, connect the battery and bulb holder with wires, as shown. Remove 1cm/½in of insulation from each end of wire. Use the paper clips to attach the wires to the battery.

2 Stir salt into a jar of water until no more dissolves. Dip the two bare wire ends into the mixture and hold them about 1cm/½in apart. Look for bubbles forming around them.

3 The bulb should light to show that electricity is passing through. Carefully sniff the jar from 20cm/8in away. What does it smell like? The smell is like swimming pools!

Heat changes

1 Make sure the pan is completely dry. Spread one teaspoonful of sugar across the bottom of the pan. Aim for a thin layer – about 5mm/¼in thick.

2 With adult supervision, place the pan over a low heat. After a few minutes, the sugar will start to melt into a thick, brown liquid. You may begin to see a few wisps of steam.

3 The sugar starts to bubble as it breaks down and gives off steam. If you continue heating the sugar, the brown, sticky liquid will change to solid black carbon.

Getting a reaction

The gas is called carbon dioxide. Ask an adult to lower a lighted match into the bowl. The flame goes out when it meets the gas.

1 Place three heaped spoonfuls of bicarbonate of soda in the bowl. Cooks often add this white powder to vegetables, such as peas and carrots. It helps to keep their natural colour.

2 Carefully pour vinegar into the bowl. As the liquid mixes with the bicarbonate of soda, a chemical reaction happens. The mixture bubbles as a gas is given off.

Tests with yeast

For thousands of years, people all over the world have used yeast for brewing beer and baking bread. Yeast is a type of fungus that lives on the skins of many fruits. Just a spoonful of yeast contains millions of separate, single-celled (very simple) organisms. Each one works like a tiny chemical factory, taking in sugar, and giving out alcohol and carbon dioxide gas. While they feed, the yeast cells grow larger and then reproduce by splitting in half.

▲ **Kneading dough**
Bread is kneaded into a soft dough and then left in a warm place to rise. The dough is then kneaded again before it is baked. This process makes the yeast produce as many bubbles of gas as possible, so that the bread is light.

Yeast turns grape juice into alcoholic wine, and makes beer from mixtures of grain and water. When it is added to uncooked dough, yeast produces gas bubbles that make the bread light and soft. Brewing and baking are important modern industries that depend on yeast working quickly.

This project consists of four separate experiments. By comparing the results, you can discover the best conditions for yeast to grow. It needs a moist environment to be active. Lack of moisture makes the cells dry out and hibernate (sleep). Add water to dried, powdered yeast, and – even after many years – it will become active again.

Finding the best conditions

YOU WILL NEED

measuring cup, water, kettle, adhesive labels, four small glass jars, teaspoon, dried yeast granules, sugar, scissors, transluscent food covering, three rubber bands, two heatproof bowls, ice cubes.

1 Half fill a kettle with water. Ask an adult to boil it for you, and then put it aside to cool. Boiling the water kills all living organisms that might stop the yeast from growing.

2 Label the glass jars, one to four. Put a level teaspoonful of dried yeast into each jar as shown here. Then put the same amount of sugar into each jar.

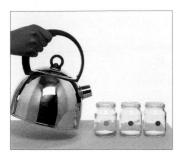

3 Pour 150ml/¼ pint/⅔ cup of the cooled water into the first three jars. Stir to dissolve the sugar. Do not pour water into the fourth jar. Put this jar away in a warm place.

4 Cut out pieces of food covering about twice a jar's width. Stretch one across the neck of each remaining jar, and secure it with a rubber band. Put the first jar in a warm place.

5 Place the second jar in a glass bowl. Put some ice cubes and cold water into the bowl. This will keep the jar's temperature close to freezing.

6 Place the third jar in another glass bowl. Pour in some hot water that is almost too hot to touch. Be careful not to use boiling water, or the jar may crack.

warm temperature

7 Regularly check all four jars over the next two hours. As the ice around the second jar melts, add more to keep the temperature low. Add more hot water to keep the third jar hot.

high temperature

cold temperature

In the jar that was kept hot, the yeast is a cloudy layer at the bottom, killed by the heat. The jar that was kept cold has only a little froth on the surface, because the cold has slowed down the yeast.

dry jar

The yeast that was kept warm has fed on the water and sugar, and its gas is pushing up the food covering. In the dry jar, there are no signs of activity, because the yeast is hibernating.

Preservation and decay

Decay is the breaking up of dead organic matter, such as animals and plants. It results when invisible creatures called bacteria, and tiny fungi called moulds, breed. The bodies of living plants and animals fight these agents of destruction, but as soon as the animals die, decay begins. Bacteria and moulds that cause decay need water to live, so decay happens best in damp conditions.

The process of preserving something aims to stop it from decaying. The ancient Egyptians were skilled at mummifying (preserving) their kings' bodies. They removed moist internal organs, such as the intestines, heart, liver and brain. Then they buried the body in natron, a kind of salt. This dried out all the fluids that speed up decay. The body was then wrapped in bandages. The bandages had been soaked in oily resins that killed bacteria and moulds in a similar way to modern antiseptic creams. You can practice slowing down and speeding up the process of decay in these two experiments.

▲ Protected by the gods
Turning the body of a great Egyptian pharaoh into a mummy was a complicated process. In addition to the preserving process, a jackal-masked priest performed sacred rituals.

peeled carrot

unpeeled carrot

plastic

stone

unpeeled apple   peeled apple

wood

What decays?

1 Peel one of the apples and one of the carrots. Line the tray with some newspaper. Add a layer of compost and place all the items on top. Add more compost to cover the items.

2 Dig a shallow hole in a shady spot and put the tray in it. Cover it with soil so that you can just see its top edges. Buried like this, the items will stay damp. Dig the tray up after a week.

Examine the results. Fruit and vegetables are attacked quickly by bacteria and moulds, especially if they have no skins. Wood takes months to decay. Stone and plastic do not decay.

Preventing decay

1 Put one slice of ordinary bread into a plastic bag, and seal it with a tie. Now toast another slice of bread until it is crispy and dry. Seal the toast in another plastic bag.

2 Spread some antiseptic cream, which is designed to kill germs, over one side of a third slice. Seal the antiseptic cream-coated third slice in another plastic bag.

3 Label each plastic bag. Leave them in a warm place and check them once a day. Bacteria and moulds are everywhere. What will they do inside your plastic bags?

▲ **Dry toast**

Look at the slices. Mould and bacteria cannot grow on the dry toast, since there is no moisture.

Do not open the bags when you have finished looking at the results. Keep the moulds and bacteria wrapped inside their plastic bags, and drop the bags into a garbage bin.

▲ **Antiseptic cream**

The chemicals in the antiseptic cream have killed any germs on the cream-covered slice of bread.

▲ **Ordinary bread**

The ordinary slice of bread is very mouldy. Mould and bacteria have thrived in the moist conditions.

Stone and concrete

Statue of Liberty

Nelson's Column

Sydney Opera House

Great Pyramid, Giza

Buildings that are made of hard stone last much longer than those made of dried earth or bricks. The people who lived in early civilizations carved stone with simple hammers and chisels – the same as you will try to do in the first experiment. When the ancient Egyptians built the pyramids more than 3,000 years ago, they had to drive large wedges into cracks in the rock face to lever off blocks of stone.

Ancient peoples used stone that they found locally, and gradually learned to use different rocks for different jobs. The Inca people of South America built with granite, a hard, igneous (volcanic) rock. The ancient Egyptians also used granite, but limestone, a softer, more easily carved sedimentary rock, was common too. Certain rocks, such as marble, were selected for decorative effects, because of their beautiful patterns and tones. Many modern buildings are made of concrete, a mixture of ground-down rocks and minerals. You can test its strength in the second experiment.

▲ Ancient scale

The Great Pyramid in Egypt is the largest stone building in the world, even though it was built over 4,000 years ago. It is made up of over 2 million blocks of stone, each of which weighs an average of 2½ tons.

Cutting and carving

1 Could you be a sculptor? Practice by marking out a simple shape on the flower-arranging foam. Use the knife to cut around it. How easy is it to use this material?

2 Now do the same with your building brick. This is much harder, but it is still softer than stone. Make sure that the knife blade is pointed away from you.

Now you know how hard it is to carve material that is much softer than stone. How long do you think it would take you to carve real stone with simple tools?

Mix your own concrete

YOU WILL NEED

rubber gloves, measuring cup, sand,

bucket, cement, gravel, water,

stirring stick, old metal tray,

small thin box, foil.

1 Place one cupful of sand in a bucket. Add two cups of cement and a handful of gravel. Take care not to touch the cement with your bare hands.

2 Add some water to the mixture, little by little. Keep stirring all the time, until the mixture has the consistency of oatmeal. Mix it well with the stick.

3 Pour the wet concrete on to a shallow metal tray and spread it out. Leave it to solidify for about half an hour. Wash all the other equipment you have used immediately.

4 Now you can shape the concrete. Make impressions of your hands, or write with the stick. The marks will be permanent once the concrete has set. Do not use your bare hands.

hand prints in concrete

5 You could make a concrete brick like those used in the construction industry. Line a small, strong box with foil. Pour in the concrete and smooth the top with the stick.

How strong is the concrete brick once it has set? Test its strength by trying to bend it. Can you rest a heavy weight on top of the brick without breaking it?

Building bridges

A platform bridge was a very early human invention, dating back tens of thousands of years. The simplest platform bridges were just a tree trunk or a single slab of stone, laid across a narrow river or steep gully, so that people could get across. Many modern platform bridges are hollow and made of steel. The model here shows how thin folded sheets make platform bridges stronger.

If you stand on a simple platform bridge, the downward force of your weight makes it sag in the middle. Too much weight can snap a flat wooden plank or crack a stone slab. As the second experiment shows, however, arch bridges do not sag when loaded. They curve up and over the gap that they span, and the forces acting on the arch squeeze it together. Weight from above is pushed outward, so that the load spreads to the side supports. The Romans were among the first to build arch bridges.

Make a platform

1 Cut out four strips of card 40 x 10cm/16 x 4in. With a ruler and pen, draw lines 1cm/½in apart across each card. Fold each card back and forth across the lines, to form zigzag pleats.

2 Lay one board flat on the table. Stand a piece of pleated card upright along the board's edges. Repeat for the other three sides. Use modelling clay to secure each corner.

3 When all sides of the platform are in place, lay the second board on top. Push downward with your hand. Pleating the card has made the platform very strong. Your platform is stronger than a platform bridge, because it is supported on four sides. Without this support, it would sag in the middle.

Make an arch

1 Although it is not shown in this picture, it would be a good idea to cover the surface with newspaper first. Place the two bricks on the work surface about 20cm/8in apart.

2 Pile sand between the bricks, and smooth it with your hands to make a curved mound. Place the wooden blocks side by side across the sand. They should touch the outer blocks.

3 The inner blocks touch each other but have V-shaped gaps between them. Mix the plaster with water until it forms a stiff paste. Use the knife to fill gaps between the blocks with paste.

5 Push down on the arch and feel how firm it is. The weight that you are putting on the bridge is supported by the two bricks at the side. This bridge is stronger than a platform bridge, and does not sag in the middle. Like stone slabs in real bridges, the wooden toy blocks make a remarkably strong curve.

4 Make sure you have filled each space where the arch meets the bricks. Wait for the plaster to dry. Once it is dry, remove the sand from underneath the arch.

toy building blocks

Tunnel construction

A tunnel has to bear the weight of millions of tons of rocks and earth – or even water – above it. One way of doing this is to make lots of brick arches that together run the length of the tunnel. An arched roof is much stronger than a flat one, because weight from above is pushed out sideways, as the first experiment shows. In the second project, you place a wedge-shaped keystone at the peak of the arch. In real life, this keystone locks the whole structure together. It compresses (squeezes) the bricks on either side, to make the arch self-supporting and very strong.

Today, a long, trainlike machine is used to bore tunnels. A big drill carves out the hole, sending the waste backwards on a conveyor belt. Behind it, robotic cranes lift precast concrete sections of the tube-shaped tunnel into place.

▲ Bridge types

The beam bridge (*top*) is made of horizontal platform supported on two or more piers (pillars). Arch bridges (*middle*) are built over steep valleys and rivers. Suspension bridges (*bottom*) support the longest bridges. The weight of the platform is carried by steel wires that hang from cables. The cables are held up by concrete towers and anchored firmly at the valley's sides.

Templates

A x 2

A x 2

27cm/10½in

33cm/13in

27cm/10½in

2cm/¾in
1.25cm/1½in
C
1.25cm/½in

2.5cm/1in
D
1cm/½in

19cm/7½in

B x 2

7cm/2¾in

21cm/8½in

6cm/2½in   6cm/2½in

Strength test

1 Place one of the pieces of cardboard on top of the building blocks. Place pebbles on top as shown above. You will see that the tunnel roof sags under the weight.

2 Curve a second piece of cardboard under the flat roof as shown. The roof supports the weight of the pebbles, because the arch supports the flat section, making it stronger.

Tunnel in a landscape

YOU WILL NEED

masking tape, two pieces of cardboard measuring 36 x 30cm/ 14½ x 12in and 46 x 27cm/ 18½ x 10½in, ruler, pencil, scissors, thin card measuring 44 x 40cm/ 17¾ x 16in, newspaper, cup of flour, ½ cup of water, acrylic paints, paintbrush, water pot, thin card (A4 size), white glue, glue brush, old sponge.

1 Tear off about four long strips of masking tape. Curve the 46 x 27cm/ 18½ x 10½in rectangle of cardboard lengthways. Use the tape to hold the curve in place.

2 Copy the two templates A on to two 36 x 30cm/14½ x 12in pieces of cardboard. Cut out the shapes. Attach each one to the sides of the tunnel, and secure with tape as shown above.

3 Fold the 44 x 40cm/17¾ x 16in thin card in half. Copy the arch template B on to the card. Cut out to make the two tunnel entrances. Stick these to the tunnel with masking tape as shown.

4 Scrunch newspaper into balls, and tape to the tunnel and landscape. Mix the flour and water to make a thick paste. Dip newspaper strips in the paste. Lay them over the tunnel.

5 Leave to dry overnight. When completely dry and hard, paint the tunnel and landscape green. Apply up to three coats, letting each one dry before you apply the next.

6 Paint the thin card to look like brick. Draw and cut out templates C and D. Draw around them on to the brick card, to make the keystone and lots of bricks. Allow paint to dry.

7 Glue the keystone at the top of the tunnel entrance. Then glue bricks around the arch at either side of the keystone. In real tunnels, there are keystones along the tunnel length.

8 Dip pieces of old sponge into green acrylic paint to make bushes. Leave to dry. Stick them on the landscape. Apply three coats of paint to the whole landscape.

The strength of a pyramid

Over a period of more than 4,500 years, people in different parts of the world built huge pyramids. The oldest Egyptian pyramids were started almost 4,600 years ago, while the youngest pyramids in Central America were finished about 600 years ago. Each one took a long time to build, sometimes over 50 years, and involved thousands of people.

Why did these civilizations opt for a pyramidal structure rather than a cube or a rectangle for their monuments? These experiments will help you to find out. In the first, by changing a cube into a pyramid, you end up with a structure that is three times taller than the original cube. A pyramid makes good use of material, by making the structure as high as possible. The second project shows that triangular shapes are more rigid than squares and do not collapse as easily. When an earthquake destroyed the Egyptian city of Cairo 700 years ago, the pyramids stood firm. Modern materials and technology make it possible to build tall, rectangular buildings that are strong and stable.

▲ **Steep challenge**
The Egyptians had no cranes to help them move the enormous slabs of stone used to build the pyramids. Workers built ramps of hard-packed earth. They hauled the slabs up these using plant-fibre ropes and wooden rollers. As the pyramid grew, the ramps became longer and steeper. When the pyramid was finished, the ramps were removed.

Bases and heights

1 Make two cubes from modelling material. The faces should measure about 3–4cm/1–1½in, but they must all be the same. Use a ruler to check your measurements.

2 Reshape one of the cubes to form a tall, square-based pyramid. Its base must be the same size as the original cube. You now have a cube and a pyramid.

3 Now measure the cube and pyramid. They have the same volume and the same size base. The pyramid is three times taller, but is strong and more stable.

4 Make the cube into a long slabs. Place the slab and the pyramid on a book. Slowly tilt the book, to imitate the effect of an earthquake. The slab topples over before the pyramid does.

5 Make another smaller cube and pyramid from modelling material. Make sure that they are the same height. Their bases must also be the same size.

6 Do the same book test with the two smaller shapes. You should still find that the pyramid is the more stable of the two shapes. It is the second of the two shapes to fall over.

A question of strength

1 For this project, you will need two models – a cube and a square-based pyramid. Make them out of large plastic drinking straws and reusable adhesive. First, make the cube.

2 After fixing four straws to make the base of your cube, you need eight more to finish it. Make sure that your cube is even, with each face the same size.

3 Now make a square-based pyramid. The base should be the same size as the base of your cube. Make the base, and just fix four more straws to it to complete your pyramid.

4 Push down gently with your hand over the middle of the cube. Move your hand slightly to one side as you push down, and you will feel the cube start to collapse.

5 Repeat this with the pyramid. You can feel how much more rigid this shape is, and it does not collapse. This is because a pyramid has triangular-shaped faces that meet at a central point.

Surveying a site

Making precise measurements in order to put up a building is called surveying. Accurate building requires two things. There must be a level base to the building, and building slabs must be laid absolutely flat, with their sides perfectly vertical, at right angles to the ground. Builders use plumb lines to check that verticals are absolutely true. A plumb line is a weight on the end of a line, which holds the line straight. These experiments show how to use water levels or a plumb line to measure differences in heights on a site.

▲ **The lie of the land**
A modern surveyor makes a detailed examination of the land before building work can start.

Is it vertical?

1 Make your own plumb line by fixing a 3cm/1¼in ball of modelling material to a piece of string. Make a large knot in the string and shape the material around it.

2 Push your stick into the ground. Make it as vertical as possible (pointing straight upwards). Keep moving it slightly, until you are sure it is straight.

3 Now use your plumb line to check how straight your stick is. Get a friend to hold the line next to the stick. Measure between the stick and line at the top and farther down. If the measurements are the same, your stick is vertical.

Is your site level?

YOU WILL NEED

Is it vertical?: non-hardening modelling material, string, a stick (about 1m/1yd long), tape measure.

Is your site level?: wooden stick 1m/1yd long, plank of wood 40 x 10cm/16 x 4in, nails, hammer, screw-in hooks, clear plastic piping (1cm/½in diameter), jug (pitcher), water dyed with ink, funnel, tape measure, wooden pole 1m/1yd long, pen.

1 Here, you are making a simple version of a surveyor's level. With adult help, nail the short plank of wood to the top of the long wooden stick. Take care with the hammer.

2 Now screw the hooks in along the bottom and up the sides of the plank. Thread the piping through the hooks. About 2cm/¾in of piping should stick up above the plank.

3 Get a friend to hold the device upright. Now, very carefully, pour the water into the pipe, using a funnel. The water level should come just above the piece of wood.

4 The friend holds the pole up 5m/5yds away. You look along the water levels so they line up, and also line up with the pole. The friend moves a finger up and down the pole. Shout when the friend's finger lines up with the water levels.

5 The friend marks this on the pole, then moves to another spot. Repeat step 4. The distance between the two marks on the pole shows the difference in level between the two places.

Powerful levers

One of the simplest and oldest gadgets in the world is the lever. Any rod or stick can act as a lever, helping to move heavy objects or prise things apart. Levers are also used for lifting, cutting, and squashing. The action of a lever can make a push more forceful, or make it a smaller push. It can also change the direction of a push. The difference between the size of the push you make on a lever (the effort) and the push the lever itself makes (the load) is called mechanical advantage.

A lever on a central pivot can also be used as a balance. The lever balances if the effect of the force (push) on one side of the pivot is the same as the effect of the force on the other. A seesaw is one sort of balancing lever. It is a plank balanced on a central post or pivot. A big person can balance someone small and light if they sit nearer to the central pivot of the seesaw.

▲ Using a simple lever
A spoon can be a lever. This girl is using the spoon as a simple lever to lift the lid off a can of paint. The lever arm pivots on the lip of the can. As the girl pushes down on the long end, the shorter end wedged under the lid lifts it up with greater force, making the stiff lid move.

▲ Cracking a nut
The strong crushing action of the nutcracker's jaws is produced by pressing the two lever arms together. A pair of nutcrackers, like a pair of scissors or a pair of pliers, has two lever arms joined at a pivot. The levers make the effort you use about four times bigger, allowing you to break the nut easily. Putting the pivot at the end of the nutcracker rather than toward the middle (as in a pair of scissors), means that the arms of the cracker can be shorter, but still create a force just as big.

lever arm

pivot

jaws

effort

load

pivot

▲ Body levers
Did you know that some parts of your body are levers? Every time you brush your hair or get up from a chair, the bones in your arms and legs act as levers. As your arm lifts up an object, your elbow is the pivot. Effort from the upper arm is transferred to your lower arm, so that you can pick up the load in your hand.

Levers and lifting

1 A ruler can be used as a lever to lift a book. With the pivot (the box) near the book, only a small effort is needed to lift the book up. The lever makes the push greater.

2 When the pivot is moved to the middle of the lever, the effort needed to lift the book up is equal to the book's weight. The effort and the load are the same.

effort

load

pivot

▲ How a lever works

A lever tilts on a pivot, which is nearer to the end of the lever with the load on it. The effort, or force, is the push you make on the long end of the lever to lift the weight of the load.

3 When the pivot is near where you are pressing, more effort is needed to lift the book. The force of the push needed to lift the book is now larger than the book's weight.

Balancing a seesaw

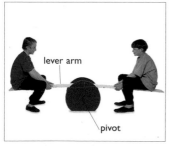

lever arm

pivot

1 Ask a friend of equal weight to sit on one side of the seesaw, while you sit on the other side. If you sit the same distance from the pivot, you make the seesaw balance.

2 Ask another friend to join you on the seesaw. By adding another person, that side of the seesaw will overbalance. The pair's greater weight will easily lift the lighter person.

3 Get the pair to move nearer to the pivot of the seesaw. Their weight can be balanced by the lighter person moving farther away from the pivot. The seesaw will be equally balanced.

Levers at work

Find out how to make three different kinds of lever in these experiments. The first is a can crusher that uses a lever action to squash a can. The second is a gripper for picking up small objects, just like a pair of tweezers. It can also work as a nutcracker. In a pair of nutcrackers, the load (in this case a grape or a nut) is between the pivot (the pencil) and the effort (where you push). In a pair of tweezers, the effort is between the pivot and the load.

The third experiment is a balance scale. It is like the ones used by the Romans about 2,000 years ago. It works by balancing the weight of an object against a known weight, in this case a bag of coins. The coins are moved along the lever arm, until they balance the object being weighed. The farther away from the pivot the weighed bag is, the greater turning effect it has on the lever arm. The heavier the weight being measured, the farther away the bag must be moved to balance the arm. The weight is read against the scale along the arm.

YOU WILL NEED

two short planks of wood about 40 x 10cm/16 x 4in and 1–2cm/½–¾in thick, hinge, screws, screwdriver, two coffee-jar lids, glue, empty can.

Can crusher

1 Lay the two planks of wood end to end. Ask an adult to help you screw them together with a hinge, using screws and a screwdriver. Make sure the hinge is secure.

2 Glue a jar lid to the inside edge of each plank of wood, with the top of the lid face down. The lids should be about halfway along each plank and the same distance from the hinge.

To crush a can, put the can in between the lids, so that it is held in place. Press down hard on the top piece of wood.

Gripper

1 Put the pencil between the two pieces of wood, near one end. Wrap the rubber bands tightly around the pieces of wood to make a pivot. You have now made the gripper.

2 Hold the gripper near the pivot to make it act like a pair of tweezers. See if you can pick up a delicate object, such as a grape, without crushing the object.

3 Hold the gripper at the end farthest away from the pivot. Now your lever operates as a pair of nutcrackers. The effort at the point you push is increased.

Balance scale

YOU WILL NEED

Gripper: short pencil, two pieces of wood each about 15cm/6in long, thick rubber bands, objects to pick up or squash, such as nuts.

Balance scale: cardboard 50 x 8cm/20 x 3in, thin card, scissors, string, ruler, hole punch, 12cm/4½in circle of card, tape, 100g/4oz of coins, felt-tipped pen, objects to weigh.

1 Make the arm by folding the cardboard in two. Make a loop of thin card and fold it loosely around the arm 11cm/4¼in from one end. Tie a piece of string to this support.

2 Make a hole 1cm/½in from the arm's end. Make the card circle into a cone. Tie it to the hole. Make an envelope from thin card, and tie it to a loop so that it hangs over the arm.

3 Put the coins in the envelope and seal it up. Starting from the middle of the support, make a mark every 5cm/2in along the arm. This scale will tell you the weight of an object.

To weigh an object, put it in the cone and slide the envelope of coins backwards and forwards along the arm, until the arm balances. Each mark along the scale equals 50g/2oz. In this picture, the object being weighed is about 75g/3oz.

The power of energy

Nothing can happen without energy. Energy is needed to do work, such as making things move. To make something move, a source of energy is needed. For example, an engine works by burning fuel – a storage of chemical energy. The two experiments here explore different ways in which energy can be captured to make something move.

The turbine experiment shows how the energy in flowing water makes a bottle spin. This energy is used in hydroelectric power stations to generate electricity. The second project shows how electrical energy from a battery spins a motor. Electric motors are used in many household appliances, such as vacuum cleaners and washing machines. The development of the steam engine and the electric motor in the 1800s provided new sources of energy that were able to power ships and railway engines, and later to light homes and streets.

▲ **Strike a light**
Lightning is a massive discharge of energy from a thundercloud. The cloud gets overloaded with electrically charged particles of water and ice.

YOU WILL NEED

scissors, plastic bottle, pencil, two wide drinking straws, plastic tape, thin string, tray, water.

3 Hold your turbine over a tray, or outdoors, so that you will not make a mess with the water. Fill the bottle with water. It will squirt out through the straws, making the bottle spin.

Turbine

1 Cut off the bottle's top with adult help. Use the pencil to poke holes around its base. Cut the straws and push them through the holes. Use tape to hold the straws in place.

2 Poke three holes around the top of the bottle. Tie three equal pieces of string through the holes, and join them to one long piece of string.

Electric motor

1 Use the bradawl to make a hole 1cm/½in from the top of each of the two end supports. Glue them to the base board, 1cm/½in inwards from the shorter edges.

3 Strip 2cm/¾in of insulation from one end of the wire and 3cm/1¼in from the other, with adult help. Wind the wire between the coil supports. Slide the reel on to the straw.

2 Cut a length of straw 12cm/4½in long. Glue the straw to one coil support. Glue the two coil support spacers to either side of the straw. Glue the second support over the top.

6 Place the magnets on the supports, so that the coil and reel spin freely. Unbend two paper clips to make hooks. Join one end of each to a connecting wire and fix to the base with thick tape. Using paper clips, join the ends of the wires to the battery, with adult supervision. The reel should start spinning around.

4 Cut a foil strip the width of the reel, to fit three-quarters of the way around the reel. Cut it in half. Put the wire ends against the reel. Tape foil over each wire so it is under the foil's middle.

5 Stick the reel to the straw. Hold it between the end supports. Slide the knitting needle through the hole in each end support. Secure the coil support with green magnet supports.

Wind and water power

Modern windmills called wind turbines are used to generate electricity. The most efficient wind turbines only have two or three blades, like the propeller of an aircraft. Sometimes just a couple of large turbines can generate enough electricity to meet all the power needs of a small community.

There are several shapes of wind turbine. One of the most efficient is the vertical-axis type. This has an axle like the dowel one in the first project. It is very efficient, because it works no matter which way the wind is blowing. The second experiment shows you how to make a water wheel that captures the energy of falling water to lift a small weight. Pour water from different heights to see if it makes a difference to the wheel's speed.

sails

simple gears

grinding stones

▲ Wind for milling

A windmill uses the power of the wind to turn heavy mill stones that grind grain to make flour. The whole building can be turned around, so that it faces into the wind. The speed of the mill is controlled by opening and closing slots in the sails. Inside a windmill is an arrangement of gear wheels, which transfers power from the sails to the grinding stones.

YOU WILL NEED

plastic bottle, scissors, tape, ruler, thin dowel, drawing pins (thumb tacks).

Make a windmill

To make the windmill spin, hold it vertically with your fingers on the thumb tacks at each end of the dowel. Blow on the vanes. The windmill will spin easily.

1 Cut the top and bottom off the bottle to leave a tube. Cut the tube in half lengthwise, then stick the two halves together in an S shape, so that the edges overlap by 2cm/¾in.

2 The piece of dowel should be about 4cm/1½in longer than the vanes. Slide it into the slot between the vanes. Press a drawing pin gently into each end of the dowel.

Make a water-wheel

1 Cut the top third off the plastic bottle. Cut a small hole in the bottom piece near the base (this is to let the water out). Cut a V-shape on each side of the rim.

2 Ask an adult to push the wire through the middle of the cork to make an axle. From the top third of the plastic bottle, cut six small curved vanes (blades) as shown.

3 Ask an adult to cut six slots in the cork with a knife. (This might be easier without the wire.) Push the plastic vanes into the slots to make the water wheel.

5 Put the water wheel on a large plate or in the sink. Pour water on to the wheel, so that it hits the upward-curving vanes. As the wheel turns, the weight should be lifted up.

4 Rest the wheel's axle in the V-shaped slots. Tape a piece of string towards one end of the axle, and tie a small weight to the end of the string. Fill a jug with water.

Energy from liquid and air

Hydraulic machines have parts that are moved by liquid. Pneumatic machines have parts that are moved by a gas such as air. A hydraulic system has a pipe filled with a liquid, such as oil, and a piston that moves to and fro within the pipe. Pushing liquid into the pipe forces the piston to move, transmitting power from one end of the pipe to the other. In a simple pneumatic system, compressed air forces a piston to move.

In the first experiment, you make a hydraulic machine powered by water pressure. Water is poured from a central reservoir (the jug (pitcher) of water) into a pipe. The water fills up a plastic bag. The bag expands and forces up the piston (the lid), which in turn raises a heavy object. Many cranes and trucks use this principle to lift heavy loads. In the air pump project, you discover the basic principles of how vacuum cleaners work. Finally, you make a miniature vacuum cleaner. Air is sucked in one hole and pushed out of another. A valve stops it from being sucked in and pushed out of the wrong holes.

◀ **Filling an empty space**
Modern vacuum cleaners have an air pump operated by an electric motor. The pump creates a vacuum inside the cleaner. Dust rushes in from the outside to fill the vacuum.

YOU WILL NEED

large plastic bottle, scissors, airtight plastic bag, plastic tube, adhesive tape, plastic funnel, spray can lid, heavy book, jug (pitcher) of water.

Make an hydraulic lifter

1 Cut the top off the large plastic bottle. Make sure the plastic bag is airtight, and wrap its neck over the end of a piece of plastic tube. Seal the bag to the tube with adhesive tape.

2 Fix a funnel to the other end of the tube. Make a hole at the base of the bottle, and feed the bag and tube through. The bag should sit in the bottom of the bottle.

3 Put the spray can lid on top of the bag, and rest a heavy book on top of the bottle. Lift the funnel end of the tube up, and slowly pour in water. What happens to the lid and the book?

Make an air pump

1 Cut around the large plastic bottle, about one third up from the bottom. Cut a slit down the side of the bottom part of the bottle, so that it will slide inside the top part.

2 Ask an adult to help you nail the bottom of the bottle to the end of a wooden stick or a piece of dowel. You have now made a piston for your air pump.

3 Cut a hole about 1cm/½in across near the neck of the bottle. Cut a piece of card about 2 x 2cm/¾ x ¾in. Tape one edge of the card to the bottle to form a flap over the hole.

4 Drop a ping-pong ball into the top part of the bottle, so that it rests in the neck. Push the bottom part of the bottle (the piston) into the top part (the cylinder).

5 Move the piston in and out, to suck air into the bottle and out of the hole. Can you see how both the valves work? The flap should automatically close when you pull the piston out.

Make a vacuum cleaner

1 Make the air pump from the project above without the card flap. Tape string to the ball, feed it through the bottle's neck, and tape it down, so that the ball is held near the neck.

2 Make a tissue paper bag and glue it over the hole near the neck of the bottle. Air from the pump will go through the bag, and anything the vacuum picks up should be trapped.

3 Try picking up tiny bits of paper with the vacuum. Pull the piston out sharply to suck the bits of paper into the bottle. Push the piston back in gently to pump the paper into the bag.

How magnets work

Magnets are usually made of the metal iron, or another material that has lots of iron in it, such as steel. Magnets can be various shapes, but all of them have the ability to pull things toward themselves. This invisible force is called magnetism. Magnets only attract (pull) metals that are made of iron or that contain iron.

Magnetism is concentrated around the poles (ends) of a magnet. A magnet has two poles, called the north pole and the south pole. The two poles may look the same but they behave differently. Put one pole of a magnet near to a pole of another magnet, and watch what happens. You may feel an attraction (pulling) force as the two poles stick together. Alternatively, you may feel a repulsion (pushing) force, as the two poles push away from each other. In all magnets, identical poles will repel (push away) each other, while different poles will pull towards each other.

Is a big magnet more powerful than a small one? Not always. You cannot tell how powerful a magnet is just by looking at it. Compare the strength and power of different magnets in the projects opposite.

▲ Seeing magnetism

You cannot see the magnetic force around a magnet, but you can see the effects of its presence when an iron nail sticks to a magnet. You can see the shape of a magnetic field by using tiny, powderlike pieces of iron, called iron filings. Iron filings reveal that the lines and strength of the magnetic force are concentrated around and between the poles at the end of the horseshoe magnet. On a bar magnet, they line up to show how the magnetic force spreads out from the poles (ends).

Tiny magnets ▶

Think of a bar of iron as having millions of micromagnets inside it. These are called domains. If they are all jumbled up, the bar is not a magnet. If the micromagnets in a bar are lined up and point the same way, it is a magnet.

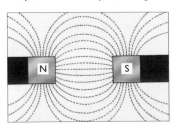

◀ Attraction and repulsion ▶

The poles of two magnets that are different or opposite will attract. Magnetic lines of force from north and south poles pull together and join. The poles of two magnets that are the same will repel or push each other apart.

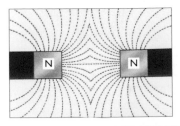

Strength of a magnet

1 Cut off a piece of tape and use it to tape the round container firmly to the work surface. The round container will act as the pivot, or the balancer.

2 Attach a magnet to one end of the ruler with a rubber band and some washers to the other end of the ruler. Position the middle of the ruler on the balancer.

3 Hold another magnet above the first. Lower it until the ruler tips over. Measure its height above the table. The higher it is when the ruler tips over, the stronger the magnet.

YOU WILL NEED

Strength of a magnet: scissors, adhesive tape, round plastic container, two magnets, ruler, rubber bands, steel washers.

Power of a magnet: pencil, drawing pins (thumb tacks), strong thread, cardboard, ruler with holes at both ends and in the middle, scissors, adhesive tape, rubber bands, adhesive dots, pen, two small bar magnets.

Power of a magnet

1 Attach one end of the thread to a pin and the other to a pencil. Draw two quarter-circles on cardboard. Make the distance from the pin to the curved edge the same as the length of the ruler.

2 Draw a triangle in one quarter-circle and cut it out. Using the triangle as a template, cut out a triangle from the other quarter-circle. Tape them together.

3 Push a tack through the ruler's end hole, so that it pivots. Attach rubber bands from the ruler's middle hole to the quarter-circle's side. Add dots labeled N and S to each ruler end.

Stand the magnet measurer upright. Attach one magnet to the ruler's top end with a rubber band. Bring the unlike pole of another magnet near it. How far can it pull the ruler? Stronger magnets pull it farther.

Magnetic Earth

The Earth behaves as if there is a giant bar magnet running through its middle from pole to pole. This affects every magnetic material that comes within its reach. If you hold a magnet so that it can rotate freely, it always ends up with one end pointing to the Earth's North Pole and the other to the South Pole. This is how a compass works – the needle automatically swings to the North. The Earth's magnetism comes from its inner core of iron and nickel.

solar wind   North Pole   lines of magnetic force

South Pole   tail of magnetosphere blown outward by solar wind

Earth

Make a compass

1 To turn the needle into a magnet, stroke the end of the magnet slowly along it. Repeat this in the same direction for about 45 seconds. This magnetizes the needle.

You can use the compass you make here to plot a magnetic field like the Earth's. The Earth's magnetic field is slightly tilted, so compasses do not swing exactly toward the North Pole, but to a point a little way off from northern Canada. This direction is known as magnetic north.

▲ Magnetic protection

The effects of Earth's magnetism extend 37,000 miles out into space. In fact, there is a vast magnetic force field around the Earth called the magnetosphere. This traps electrically charged particles and so protects the Earth from the solar wind – the deadly stream of charged particles hurtling from the Sun.

2 Place the magnetized needle on the slice of cork. Make sure that it is exactly in the middle, otherwise it will not spin evenly. Tape the needle into place.

3 Fill the bowl nearly to the brim with water, and float the cork in it. Make sure the cork is exactly in the middle and can turn without rubbing on the edges of the bowl.

The Earth's magnetic field should now swivel the needle on the cork. One end of the needle will always point to the north. That end is its north pole.

Magnetic field

YOU WILL NEED

Make a compass: steel needle, bar magnet, slice of cork, adhesive tape, small bowl, water.

Magnetic field: large sheet of paper, bar magnet, your needle compass from the first project, pencil.

1 Lay a large sheet of paper on a table. Put the magnet in the middle of the paper. Set up your needle compass a few centimetres/an inch or two away from one end of the magnet.

2 Wait as the compass needle settles in a particular direction as it is turned by the magnet. Make a pencil mark on the paper to show which way it is pointing.

3 Move the compass a little way toward the other end of the magnet. Mark a line on the paper to show which way the needle is pointing now.

4 Repeat Step 3 for about 25 different positions around the magnet. Try the compass both near the magnet and farther away. You should now have a pattern of marks.

Look at the pattern of marks you have made on the paper. They should form a series of rings around the magnet, like layers of an onion. Earth's magnetic field is shaped like this.

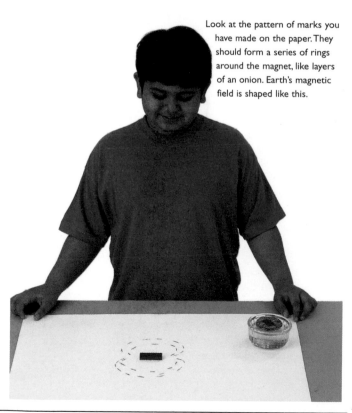

Magnets and maps

Look at a map – which way up does it go? Maps are important. They let us know our location. Without magnets, we would not know how to use a map or find our way around an area. Compass needles are tiny magnets that rotate to point to the Earth's magnetic north. Look on a local map to find a diagram of the compass points, an arrow, or 'N' that indicates north. Then set a compass so that the needle points north. Turn the map so that its north faces the same way as the compass north. Now the map is lined up accurately in relation to the landscape. If you are on a hilltop with wide views, you can see how the map is a tiny plan of the countryside around.

▲ Magnetic migration

The yellow arrows show the migration routes of the Arctic tern. The routes follow the Earth's magnetic force. The tern flies from north to south and then, later in the year, from south to north. Birds may also use rivers, mountains, coastlines, the Sun, Moon and stars to help them find their way.

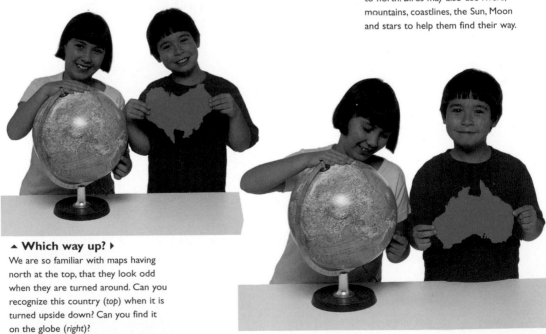

▲ Which way up? ▶

We are so familiar with maps having north at the top, that they look odd when they are turned around. Can you recognize this country (*top*) when it is turned upside down? Can you find it on the globe (*right*)?

Loop compass

1 Straighten out a paper clip. Magnetize it by stroking it with the strong magnet. Cut a circle of card, bend the wire into a large loop, and insert it into holes in the card.

2 Tape the paper clip to the piece of cork and to the card circle. Tie the thread to the top of the wire loop. Let it hang and twirl around freely. It is now ready to test.

3 Does the paper clip magnet work as a compass needle and point north and south? Check it with the store-bought compass. What do you find happens?

Drawing a maze

YOU WILL NEED

Loop compass: paper clip, strong magnet, thin card, scissors, thin wire, adhesive tape, cork tile, thread, store-bought compass.

Drawing a maze: cardboard, coloured pens, compass.

1 Draw a maze on cardboard. Make it vibrant and fun. Put in some dead ends and false turns. Make sure one route leads all the way through from one end of the maze to another!

2 Record your course through the maze, using compass points for the direction. You can limit the information to north, south, east and west or include northeast, southwest and so on.

Can you find your way through this maze? When you have made it to the other side, try recording your route with compass points. At the beginning of the journey, you head east, turn north and then go east again. Can you complete these instructions for the entire journey?

Electric magnets

wires carrying electricity

case wire coil

magnet

frame

moving cone

Some magnets, such as bar and horseshoe magnets, are permanent. They have what scientists call "spontaneous permanent magnetism." Their magnetism needs no outside force or energy to create it. A way of making magnetism is by using electricity. When electricity flows through a wire or another similar conducting (carrying) material, it produces a magnetic field around the wire. This is called electromagnetism or EM. In fact, magnetism and electricity are very closely linked. Each can be used to make the other. EM is used in many tools, machines and devices. Some electromagnetic machines use the electricity from batteries. Others need the much more powerful mains electricity from wall sockets.

The first practical electromagnets were made by the British bootmaker and spare-time scientist, William Sturgeon. He used them to amaze audiences at his science shows in the 1820s. The basic design has hardly changed since. You can make a similar electromagnet in the projects.

▲ Loudspeaker

Electrical signals are transferred to the loudspeaker along a connecting wire (speaker lead). Electricity flows through the wire coil, which is attached to the plastic speaker cone. The signals make the coil into an electromagnet that varies in strength. This magnetic field is itself inside the field of a strong permanent magnet. The two fields interact, with like poles repelling. This makes the coil move or vibrate, and the loudspeaker cone vibrates, too. This in turn sends out sound waves.

▶ Creating a magnetic field

As electricity flows through a wire, a magnetic field is created around it. The magnetic lines of force flow in circles around the wire. This is called an electromagnetic field. As soon as the electricity is switched off, the magnetism stops.

◀ Seeing electromagnetism

If iron filings are sprinkled on to a piece of cardboard that has an electricity-carrying wire through it, the filings are affected by the magnetic field. They arrange themselves in circles to show the lines of magnetic force, as they do with an ordinary magnet.

▼ Are you receiving me?

The earpiece of a telephone receives varying electrical signals from the mouthpiece of the telephone held at other end of the line. The earpiece works like a simple loudspeaker to recreate the sounds of the speaking person's voice.

diaphragm (thin sheet)

magnets

wire coil

Electromagnet

1 Using the wire strippers and with close adult supervision, carefully remove 2.5cm/1in plastic insulation from each end of the wire. These bare ends will connect to the battery.

2 Carefully wrap the wire into a tight coil around the iron nail. The plastic insulation around the wire conducts the electricity around the iron nail.

3 With close adult supervision, connect the wire's ends to the battery terminals. There may be a small spark, so take great care. Test the electromagnet by picking up paper clips.

Adding a switch

YOU WILL NEED

Electromagnet: wire strippers, 2m/2yds of wire (insulated, plastic-coated, multistrand copper), large iron nail, 9-volt battery, paper clips.

Adding a switch: hole punch, piece of thin card, brass fasteners.

---

1 Make two equal holes in the piece of card. Push the brass fasteners into them. Push one of the fasteners through a paper clip first. Open out the legs of the fasteners.

2 With adult supervision, connect one end of electromagnet wires to the fastener. Connect the other to a battery terminal. Attach the remaining fastener to the other terminal with short wire. Turn the card over.

screen

electrical plates have a magnetic field

electron guns

beam is bent by field

▲ Inside a television
Television sets, computer monitors and other similar screens have electromagnet-type devices inside. These are usually shaped like flat plates. They bend the beam that scans across the screen line by line, to build up the picture. This occurs many times every second.

3 Push the paper clip attached to one fastener away from the other fastener. No electricity flows. Turn the clip to touch the fastener. Electricity flows, switching on the electromagnet.

Computer data storage

The hard disc of a computer consists of a number of flat, circular plates. Each one of these plates is coated with tiny magnetic particles. The hard disc also contains a controlling mechanism called the read/write head. This is positioned slightly above the magnetic plates. Data (information) is sent to the disc as a series of electrical pulses. These are sent to the read/write head, which contains a tiny electromagnet. The head magnetizes the tiny magnetic particles on the surface of the plates. This pattern of particles on the disc represents the data. You can see how this happens in the project.

When reading information, the magnetized particles on the hard disc create a small current in the head as the plates spin under it. This is then converted by circuits into binary code, a number system that computers use. The code is based on just two numbers (binary means two), 0 and 1. Different combinations represent the letters of the alphabet.

central point around which the discs spin

read/write h

magnetic plates store information

hard drive inside the computer

▲ Inside the hard drive
A typical drive consists of a stack of thin discs, called a platter. The upper surface of each disc is coated with tiny magnetic particles, and each disc has its own read/write head on a movable arm. When storing and reading information, the discs spin at very high speeds (up to 120 revolutions a second).

Input devices

mouse

keyboard

scanner

Storage devices

hard drive

CDs and DVDs   memory stick

Processing

Output devices

printer

monitor

speakers

◄ Using computers
When people use a computer, they are doing four different things:

1. Inputting data (information) using an input device, such as a mouse, keyboard or scanner.

2. Storing the data on a hard drive, CDs, DVDs or a memory stick so that it can be reused.

3. Working with the data they put in (often called processing).

4. Retrieving and looking at the data using an output device, such as a printer, monitor or speakers.

Storing data on disc

1 Draw a circle with a diameter of 20cm/8in on the piece of card. Draw three more circles inside, each with a diameter 2cm/¾in smaller than the one before. Cut out the largest circle.

2 Position a ruler at the middle of the circle where the compass point has made a hole. Draw four lines through the middle to divide the circle into eight equal parts.

3 Use a red marker to shade in six or seven sections as shown above. Leave the remaining section white. The white areas represent full disc space. Red areas are empty disc space.

4 Attach some modelling material to the rim of a plastic cup. Then turn it upside down on a smooth surface. Press it down gently to make sure it is secure. Place the circle on top.

5 Push the drawing pin through the middle of the circle into the cup. Make sure the circle can turn. Put paper clips on the surface. Hold the magnet under the circle. Move it around.

The paper clips will move around the surface of the circle, and all line up in one section of the circle. This is what happens to the magnetic particles on a hard disc when an electric current is passed through them by the read/write head. In a computer, the way the magnetic particles line up is a record of the data stored on the hard disc. Remove the paper clips from the circle. Spin it clockwise with one hand, and with a finger of the other hand, touch areas of the circle. If you stop the circle on a white part, you have found data. If you stop on a red section, you have found empty disc space.

Fun with magnets

Many tricks rely on the invisible power of magnets. For example, did you know that you can remove paper clips from water without getting your fingers wet? The first project shows you how to make a paper bat that hovers in mid air.

Magnets are used to recover pieces of wrecked ships from awkward and dangerous places on the sea bed, where the water might be murky. The magnetic fishing game here demonstrates how magnets are used in this way.

▲ **Floating trick**
Put paper clips in a beaker of water, and slide the magnet up the side. The paper clips will follow, dragged along by the magnet, until they reach the rim.

YOU WILL NEED

Bat magnet: black paper, white pencil, scissors, stiff paper, adhesive tape, stiff wire, string, paper clips, strong magnet.

Magnetic fishing: different coloured plastic bags, felt-tipped pen, scissors, paper clips, magnets, string, wooden dowel, adhesive tape, deep plate or shallow bowl, water, jug (pitcher) or watering can.

Bat magnet

1 Draw a large bat shape on to a sheet of black paper with the white pencil. (You could fold the paper in half first to make sure that your bat is symmetrical.) Cut out the bat shape.

2 Tape pieces of stiff paper to the bat's underside, as shown. Then tape lengths of stiff wire across each of the wings. Secure the wire with a piece of string.

3 Place several paper clips on the pieces of paper that you have used to stiffen the bat. Cover each paper clip with a piece of tape to keep it secure.

Lift the bat from the top side with the magnet by attracting the paper clips through the paper. As the bat rises, the string lengthens. Can you lift the magnet so that the bat hovers in mid-air?

Magnetic fishing

1 Draw some fish shapes on to the plastic bags with the felt-tipped pen. Keep the bags as still as possible while you do this. Cut out the shapes carefully with the scissors.

2 Decorate each of the fish with the pen. Draw scales and a face on one side of each fish, and write a different number on the other side of each fish.

3 Attach a steel paper clip to each fish. Make sure the paper clips are firmly attached. This will allow you to catch the fish with a magnetic rod.

4 Tie a magnet to one end of a piece of string. If you tie the string around the middle of the magnet, it will be very secure and the magnet won't fall out.

5 Tape the string that is attached to the magnet, to the end of some wooden dowel with tape. Make sure it is fixed on securely, or it may float off in the water.

6 Put all of your fish, scale side up, in a plate or bowl, and fill with water from a jug or watering can. You are now ready to start the fishing game.

WARNING!

Keep plastic bags away from small children as they can be very dangerous.

Lower your fishing rods into the water to catch the fish. The paper clips will be attracted to the magnets on the ends of the rods. Lift your fish out of the pond. When there are no fish left, count up the points on the back of your fish, and the highest score wins.

Magnet sports

You can make your own table-top car race, using some magnets. Small, flat bar and ring magnets are best. The trick is to stay on the track and speed along, but not so fast that the magnet loses your car! If that happens, the race is over. The second project shows you how to create your own Olympic Games using an electromagnet. A washer represents a discus, a nut a shot put and a nail a javelin. Use the electromagnet to throw each of them. When you switch off the electromagnet, it releases the iron or the steel object.

Magnetic racing

1 Carefully glue a magnet to the end of each ruler or strip of wood. Use 30cm/12in rulers if you can, or if these are unavailable, use similar-sized strips of wood.

2 Draw the shapes of some racing cars on the card. You can make the wheels a different tone and maybe add stripes, too, so that each car looks different.

3 Carefully cut out the racing car shapes with scissors. Decorate the cars with stick-on shapes, such as stars, to make up your own racing team.

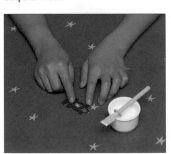

4 Glue a steel paper clip to the underside of each racing car. Let the glue dry thoroughly while you draw a racing track on a large sheet of cardboard.

Put the track on two books, so it is raised all around the edges. Place your racing cars on the start line. Push the ruler underneath, so the magnet faces upwards and attracts the paper clip on the base of your car. Move the ruler slowly, so the magnet drags the paper clip and car along. Practice driving like this for a while before you race your opponent.

Electromagnetic Olympics

YOU WILL NEED

sheets of thin card, scissors, white glue, glue spreader, adhesive tape, felt-tipped pen, decorative stick-on shapes, large iron nail, insulated (plastic-coated) copper wire, wire strippers, battery, paper clip, washer, small nails, nut.

1 Cut a sheet of card into a base about 50 x 40cm/20 x 16in. Cut four strips the same length and 10–15cm/4–6in deep, for the sides. Glue the sides and base together.

2 Cut out squares of card for the scoreboard, and tape them together to make a sheet that will fit neatly into the box. Write numbers on them and decorate them.

3 Fit the scoreboard into the box. It is best not to glue it, since you may wish to take it out and change the scores, or make a new scoreboard as you become an expert at the games.

4 Cut two more card strips. Tape them together at each of their short edges. Glue the other short edges inside the box, on opposite sides. Position this "arch" at one end of the box.

5 Make an electromagnet from the nail and wire. Tape it to the arch, so it hangs below by its wires. Connect the free ends of the wire to the battery. Use a paper clip as a battery switch.

Push the nail that hangs below the wires to test that it swings back and forth. Switch on the nail electromagnet using the paper clip switch. It should attract an iron or steel object, such as the nail, which is the javelin. Push the nail electromagnet so it swings back and forth. Turn off the switch, and the javelin will be released. Note where this lands on the scoreboard.

Images from light

The picture on a television screen is made up of thin lines of light. In the first project, you will see that a television picture is made up from rows of dots of coloured light. The picture consists of just three colours – red, green and blue. Viewed from a distance, these mix to produce a full range of colours – as the second experiment demonstrates. Plasma screens work in a similar way, although instead of using a cathode ray tube the image is produced by passing a current across a gas (plasma) to produce ultraviolet photons. These are translated into visible red, green and blue light when they interact with a phosphor layer on a sheet of glass.

Fax machines and scanners work in a similar way to television. When you insert a sheet of paper, a beam of light moves back and forth across it and sensors read the paper. This information is then changed into a code and either sent down a phone line, in the case of a fax, or to a computer, in the case of a scanner. At the receiving end, the code is translated into dots, which are either printed to produce a facsimile (copy) of the original or appear on a computer screen as an image.

screen

cathode ray tube

electron beam

▲ **Tube travel**
The cathode ray tube is the heart of a television. Pictures are received in the form of electrical impulses. These impulses control a stream of electrons inside the cathode ray tube. The electron beam scans across the screen and creates the pictures as points of coloured light. This is the picture that the viewer sees.

TV screen

YOU WILL NEED

TV screen: TV set, torch (flashlight), powerful magnifying glass.

Secondary colours: red, green, and blue transparent plastic sheet, three powerful torches (flashlights), three rubber bands, thin black card.

Digital images: ruler, pencil, tracing paper, photograph, black felt-tipped pen.

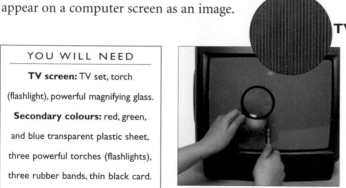

1 Turn off the TV. Shine the torch close to the screen and look through the magnifying glass. You will see that the screen is covered in very fine lines.

2 Turn on the TV and view the screen through the magnifying glass. The picture is made up of minute rectangles of light coloured red, green and blue.

Secondary colours

1 Attach a piece of coloured plastic over the end of each of your three torches. Stretch the plastic tightly, and use a rubber band to hold it firmly in place.

2 Turn on the torches on to the black card. You can see the three different primary colours of red, green and blue on the black card.

3 Position the torches so that the three circles of coloured light overlap in a clover leaf pattern. Overlapping colours mix to give new, secondary colours.

Digital images

1 Draw lines 5mm/¼in apart to cover the tracing paper in squares. Put the paper over the photograph. Use the pen to fill each dark square. Leave each light square blank.

The picture is made from squares that are either black or white.

The result is a "digitized" image, which means it can be represented by numbers – the digit 1 for white squares, and the digit 0 for black squares. The digitized image contains less detail than the original photo. You could increase the detail of the image by using a greater number of smaller squares.

A photographic image on film

Having created a focused image of a scene, a camera must have some way of recording the image. This is the job of the film or, in the case of digital cameras, the silicon chip that is covered in light-sensitive spots called photosites.

Film is coated with chemicals that are affected by light. When an image strikes the film, the coating records the patterns of light, dark and colour. Film has to be developed with chemicals before you can see the recorded pictures. Digital cameras, however, record the image electronically as binary code (0s and 1s), which needs to be translated into an image by a computer. So, for this project, film is a better way of showing how light can affect chemicals and produce a picture.

It does not matter if you do not have a film camera, as you do not need one to see how film works. In fact, you do not even need a film! You can use black and white photographic paper instead. Photographic paper is the paper that prints are made on. It works in the same way as film. Here, you can see how to make a picture called a photogram by covering some parts of a sheet of photographic paper with objects and then shining light on the sheet. When the paper is developed, the areas that were hit by the light turn black, leaving you an image of the objects.

YOU WILL NEED

developer for paper (not film) and fixer (both from a photographic supplier), rubber gloves, protective glasses, plastic dishes, desk lamp, photographic paper, different-shaped objects, such as keys and scissors, plastic tongs.

▲ Danger!
This symbol, on photographic chemical bottles, means that they can be dangerous if not used with care. Always wear protective gloves and goggles.

◄ Photographic paper
For black and white prints, you need a paper called monochrome paper. Buy the smallest size you can, and choose grade 2 if possible, with a gloss (shiny) finish. The paper comes in a light-proof envelope or box. Only open the envelope in complete darkness. The paper is in a second, black polyurethene envelope. You will also need two photographic chemicals – developer for paper (not film) and fixer. Buy them from a photographic supplier, and ask an adult to help you use them safely.

Make your own photogram

1 Ask an adult to help you follow the instructions to dilute the chemicals with water. Protect your eyes and hands when handling them. Store the diluted chemicals in plastic bottles.

2 Turn off the lamp. Lay a sheet of photographic paper down, shiny side up. Put some objects on it. Then turn the lamp on again for a few seconds.

3 Pick up the paper with the tongs, and put it into the dish of developer. Push the paper down, so that it is completely underneath the liquid.

4 After a minute, use the tongs to move the paper into the fixer. Leave the paper right under the liquid for a minute, until the image is fixed.

images made on
photographic paper

5 Now you can turn the light back on. Using the tongs, lift the paper out of the fixer and wash it with running water for a few minutes. Then lay the paper on a flat surface to dry. This technique is an excellent way of producing unique invitations and greetings cards quickly and effectively.

Getting in focus

Before taking a photograph, you need to make sure that your subject is in focus. When it is, all the rays of light that leave a point on the subject are bent by the lens, so that they hit the correct place on the film or silicon chip. This makes a clear, sharp image. Parts of the scene inside or behind the subject may not be in focus. On some cameras, you have to choose the part of the scene that you want to be in focus. Autofocus cameras focus the lens by automatically choosing the object at the middle of the image to be taken.

This experiment involves making a simple camera with just a few basic pieces of equipment. It uses photographic paper (paper with a light-sensitive coating on one side) instead of film, and a pinhole instead of a lens. When the paper is processed, you will have a negative. The "Easy prints" project on the next page shows you how to develop it.

viewfinder
lens
pentaprism
light ray
mirror

▲ Focusing SLRs
With an SLR (single lens reflex) camera, you can see exactly what the image looks like through the viewfinder. On a manual-focus SLR, you turn a ring around the lens until your subject comes into focus. When the subject is in focus, the light rays meet on the film focal plane. This is the exposed part of the film that is held flat at the back of the camera by a pressure plate. You can see it if you open the back of your camera when it is empty.

YOU WILL NEED

pinhole box viewer, foil, scissors, adhesive tape, pencil, black paper, thin card, ruler, heavy light-proof cloth or plastic sheet, photographic paper, rubber band.

◄ Get it sharp
In this photograph (*left*), the subject is in sharp focus. You can see all the fine detail. When the same shot is out of focus (*below*), it makes the subject look blurred. Autofocus cameras focus on the object in the middle of the viewfinder and do the job of focusing for you.

Making a pinhole camera

I Make the pinhole viewer from the "Make your own viewer" project, but remove the tracing-paper screen. Replace the 4cm/1½in card square with foil.

2 Pierce a hole, 2mm/⅟₁₆in across, in the middle of the foil using a sharp pencil. Open the back of the box. Roll up some black paper, and fit it through the large hole to line the inside.

3 Cut a square of card large enough to completely cover the foil. Tape just the top edge of the square of card to the box, so that it will act as a shutter.

4 Measure and cut a square of card to fit across the other end of the box. Tape it to one edge, so that it closes over the hole like a door or flap.

5 Lay the heavy, light-proof cloth or light-proof plastic sheet on the working surface. Cut a piece of the cloth or sheet large enough to fold around the end of the box.

winding arm

viewing window

lenses

film

light

▲ Reflex action

In a single lens reflex camera, light enters through the lenses at the front and strikes the film at the back. Users can see clearly what they are photographing by means of a prism mounted in the camera.

6 In a completely dark room, and feeling with your fingers, put a piece of the photographic paper underneath the flap at the end of the box.

7 Close the flap, then, still feeling with your fingers, wrap the cloth or plastic sheet tightly over it. Next, put a rubber band tightly around the box to secure it.

8 Now you can turn the light on. Point the camera at a well-lit object and open the shutter. Leave the camera perfectly still for about five minutes, and then close the shutter.

Letting in the light

Exposure is the word for the amount of light that reaches the film or silicon chip in your camera. The aperture (opening) is a hole behind the lens that can be adjusted to let more or less light. Changing the aperture affects both the brightness of an image and the depth of field that is in focus. Your eyes work in the same way. If the light is bright, your pupils get smaller to protect your retinas. If the light is dim, then the pupils enlarge to let in more light. In the experiment opposite you can investigate different apertures for yourself.

One of the first things photographers want to do is to get their films developed or view the image on the camera, so that they can see how the pictures have turned out. If you have just taken a photograph with the pinhole camera you made in an earlier project, you can find out how easy it is to turn it into a photographic print in the project below.

> **YOU WILL NEED**
>
> **Easy prints:** photographic paper and chemicals, negative from pin-hole camera, torch (flashlight) or desk lamp, safety glasses, rubber gloves, plastic dishes, plastic tongs or tweezers.
>
> **Amazing apertures:** magnifying glass, cardboard tube, adhesive tape, scissors, thin card, tracing paper, desk lamp.

▲ **How does a shutter work?**
Open the back of your camera (when there is no film inside). Place a small strip of tracing paper where your film usually goes. Aim the camera at a subject and press the shutter release button. You should see a brief flash of the image on your tracing paper.

Easy prints

1 In a totally dark room, lay a fresh sheet of photographic paper on a flat surface, shiny side up. Lay the negative from your pinhole camera face down on top.

2 Shine a torch or a desk lamp on the top of the two papers for a few seconds. Turn the light off, and remove your paper negative. Put on the safety glasses and gloves.

3 Put the fresh paper into a tray of developing fluid, then fix and wash the paper (see the project on "Making your own photogram"). You should end up with a print of the original image.

Amazing apertures

1 Make sure that your magnifying glass fits into your cardboard tube. Then carefully attach the magnifying glass to one end of the tube using small pieces of adhesive tape.

2 Roll a piece of thin card around the other end of the cardboard tube. Tape the top edge down so that it makes another tube that slides on and off the first one.

3 Cut out a circle of tracing paper with a diameter the same as the sliding card tube. Use tape to attach it across the end of the tube. This will form your viewing screen.

4 With the viewing screen facing toward you, aim your tube at a desk lamp that is turned on. Can you see an image of the bulb on the screen?

6 Cut a hole (about 5mm/¼in wide) in a piece of card, to make a small aperture. Look at the light bulb again and hold the card in front of the lens. The smaller aperture will bring the light bulb into focus. Is it clearer? Can you read the writing on the bulb?

5 Slide the tubes slowly together, until the image of the bulb is clear and in focus. Now adjust the tubes again so that the image is slightly out of focus.

How telescopes work

Optical telescopes use lenses or mirrors to make distant objects look bigger and brighter. Lens telescopes are also called refractors. Mirror telescopes are called reflectors. Most large astronomical telescopes for looking at stars are reflectors.

eyepiece lens

starlight

primary mirror reflects an upside-down image

secondary mirror corrects image

The first experiment shows you how to make a reflecting telescope, using a mirror. A reflecting telescope's main mirror is curved, so that light rays bounce off at an angle.

The refracting telescope in the second experiment uses lenses. There are difficulties involved in making big lenses, which is why most of the telescopes used in astronomy are reflectors. Our brains work out how big an object is by analyzing the angle of the light rays from it as the rays enter our eyes. Telescopes use lenses or mirrors to change this angle. Bending light rays from distant objects makes them seem larger than they would appear to the naked eye.

▲ **Reflecting telescope**
Light reflects off the primary mirror. The light rays bounce off a small secondary mirror, and are focused and magnified by an eyepiece lens. Astronomers use telescopes to help them study the stars and other planets. Telescopes are often built on top of mountains, for the clearest views. There, the air is thin and there are no lights from towns. The William Herschel Telescope (WHT) is located 2,400m/8,000ft above sea level on top of an extinct volcano on La Palma, in the Canary Islands.

Make a single-mirror reflecting telescope

1 Draw a circle around the front of the desk lamp on a sheet of purple paper. Cut it out. Then cut out an arrow in the middle. Stick the circle on to the front of the lamp.

2 Set up the desk lamp and mirror so that the mirror reflects the light from the lamp on to a nearby wall. Use modelling material to help support the mirror, if necessary.

3 Set up the magnifying glass, so that light reflecting from the mirror passes through it. The lens magnifies and focuses the light, projecting an upside-down arrow.

Make a refracting telescope

1 Draw around the front of the desk lamp on a sheet of red paper. Using scissors, cut out a star in the middle of the circle. Then cut out the circle, as shown.

2 Using tape, fasten the circle of paper securely over the front of the desk lamp. Make sure that it does not touch the bulb, because this could cause the paper to burn.

3 Position the desk lamp so that it shines on a nearby wall. Adjust the angle of the lamp if necessary. Make sure that the lamp's base is stable, to prevent it from tipping over.

4 Position a magnifying glass between the lamp and the wall. To support the glass and fix it in place, take the handle and wedge it firmly in a lump of modelling material.

5 Turn on the lamp. Adjust the magnifying glass, so that the light passing through it appears as a blurred patch of light on the wall. The glass acts like a telescope's objective lens.

6 Position the second lens behind the first lens. This acts as an eyepiece lens. Adjust the eyepiece lens, until the light is focused to form the sharp image of the star.

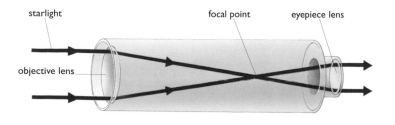

starlight   focal point   eyepiece lens

objective lens

▲ Refracting telescope

Light from a distant star passes through the objective lens. The light rays from distant objects change direction as they enter the lens, and again as they leave it. A magnified, blurry image of the star appears. The image is brought into focus by the lens in the eyepiece.

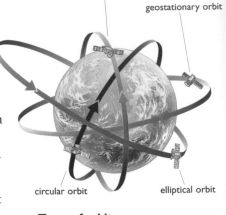

polar orbit

geostationary orbit

circular orbit

elliptical orbit

Satellites and orbits

The movement of a satellite around the Earth is fixed in either a circular or an elliptical (oval) orbit. The satellite can be positioned in a polar orbit, circling the Earth from pole to pole, or placed in an equatorial orbit around the Equator, or in any orbit in between. It may cross the sky several times a day in a low Earth orbit (LEO), or it may hang in one place, in geostationary orbit. In the first project you can see for yourself how geostationary orbits work.

The type of orbit is chosen according to the job the satellite is there to do. Most communications and weather satellites are placed in geostationary orbit 36,000km/22,000 miles above the Equator. A satellite in this orbit keeps pace with the turning Earth, and appears to hang motionless over the same spot on the ground. Once a radio dish on the ground is aimed at the satellite, the dish need not be moved again. Other satellites have to be tracked using movable radio dishes that follow the satellite as it crosses the sky. The second project demonstrates the way in which satellites relay signals from one place to another.

▲ Types of orbits
Weather satellites are often placed in geostationary orbits. They always face the same part of the Earth. Polar orbits are often chosen for scientific-survey satellites. As the satellite orbits from pole to pole, the Earth turns below it. In time, the satellite passes over every point on the Earth's surface.

> ### YOU WILL NEED
> 15 strips of thin blue card, 30 strips of thin red card, rope, a friend.

Geostationary orbit

1 Use the card strips to mark a blue circle, with a larger red circle around it on the ground. Hold one end of the rope, and ask a friend to hold the other end.

2 Walk around the inner circle, while your friend walks around the outer circle. The blue inner circle represents the Earth, and the outer circle represents the orbit of a satellite around the Earth. If your orbiting friend keeps pace with you as you walk, your human satellite is in a geostationary orbit.

Make a satellite relay

I Using the scissors, cut out a
rectangle of blue paper just big
enough to wrap around the tin can.
Tape it in place. The tin can will act as
a ground-based radio receiver.

2 Measure out a 10 x 10cm/4 x 4in
piece of card with the ruler. Cut it
out and stick it to one side of the tin
can. This will act as an antenna on your
tin-can receiver.

3 Place the tin can on the floor. Take
the long ruler and lay it on the
floor directly in front of the tin can.
Place it on the opposite side to the
antenna, as shown.

4 Place the mirror on the ruler
about 75cm/2½ft from the tin can.
The mirror will act like a satellite in
geostationary orbit relaying signals.
Fix in place with modelling material.

5 Darken the room. Place the torch
beside the can, as shown. The torch
will send out light beams in the same
way that a ground-based transmitter
sends out radio waves.

6 Switch on the torch. Move the
mirror along the yardstick. Keep
moving it, until the light beams are
reflected off the mirror satellite and
on to the antenna of the tin can.

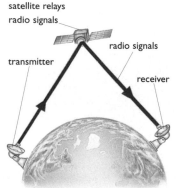

satellite relays
radio signals

radio signals

transmitter

receiver

◄ **Redirecting radio waves**
Comsats (communication satellites) in
geostationary orbit above the Equator
allow radio transmissions to be sent to
anywhere on the Earth's surface. Radio
signals are transmitted from one side
of the planet, and aimed at the orbiting
satellite. The comsat then relays
(redirects) the signal to a receiver on
the opposite side of the Earth.

Power boost in Space

Some space probes, including *Pioneer 10* and *11*, used gravity boosts to help them travel through the Solar System. To get a boost, a probe passes by a planet and becomes attracted by its gravity. It is pulled by the planet on its orbit around the Sun. Some of the planet's orbital speed is transferred to the probe, which is then catapulted toward the next planet to be visited. This slingshot effect is vital, as robot spacecraft would not be able to carry enough fuel to change course from planet to planet. The first project shows how the slingshot effect works. Space probes send back information to Earth by radio signals. These are collected by large dish antennae on Earth. The second project shows why many of the radio antennae used are dish-shaped.

▼ Pioneering probes

Probes have landed on or flown past almost every planet in the Solar System. The most widely traveled deep space probes are *Pioneer 10* and *11*, and *Voyager 1* and *2*, which have toured most of the Solar System's outer planets. They used the pull of gravity from each planet they passed to change their course and send them to the next planet. *Pioneer 10* flew past Jupiter, and the flight path of the *Pioneer 11* probe took it past Jupiter and then to Saturn.

YOU WILL NEED

two thick books (of equal thickness), 60 x 30cm/24 x 12in piece of cardboard, marble-sized steel ball, strong magnet, adhesive tape, two 30cm/12in lengths of wooden dowel.

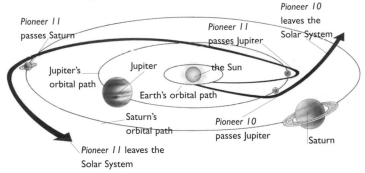

Pioneer 11 passes Saturn

Jupiter's orbital path

Jupiter

the Sun

Earth's orbital path

Saturn's orbital path

Pioneer 11 passes Jupiter

Pioneer 10 leaves the Solar System

Pioneer 10 passes Jupiter

Saturn

Pioneer 11 leaves the Solar System

Gravity boost

1 Place the books flat on a table about 15cm/6in apart. Lay the piece of cardboard on top of the books, then roll the steel-ball space probe across it. It moves smoothly across the surface.

2 Place the magnet under the cardboard. Roll the steel-ball probe across the cardboard. It is drawn toward the magnet planet by the gravitylike pull of its magnetic field.

3 Tape the magnet to the dowel. Roll the ball and then pull the magnet away. The ball speeds up and is pulled along by the magnet planet, like a probe getting a gravity boost.

radio energy

secondary mirror reflects radio energy to receiver

reflector dish

pivot allows dish to tilt

receiver

revolving base

POWER BOOST IN SPACE

◀ Beaming waves

Dish antennae reflect their collected radio energy back to the receiver. Space probes use their antennae to receive radio signals from mission control on Earth. The receiver can also act as a transmitter, allowing the probe to send back its findings to Earth.

YOU WILL NEED

plain postcard, pencil, ruler, scissors, 60 x 100cm/2 x 3ft piece of cardboard, non-hardening modelling material, 20 x 50cm/8 x 20in strip of mirror board, torch (flashlight).

Make a dish antenna

1 Draw nine thin slits on the postcard using the pencil and ruler. Each slit should measure 2.5cm x 0.5mm/1 x ¼in. They should be equally spaced out from each other, 5mm/¼in apart.

2 Using the scissors, carefully cut out the slits in the postcard. The slits in the card will filter light, splitting it up into thin rays that will reflect off the curve of the antenna.

3 Place the large piece of thick cardboard on a table. Stand the postcard 40cm/16in from one end of the card, with the slits facing down. Fix it in position with modelling material.

4 Bend the reflective mirror board to form a semicircular antenna, as shown. Stand it at one end of the thick cardboard base. Then fix it firmly in position using modelling material.

5 Switch on the torch. Direct the light beam, so that it shines through the slits in the postcard. The light is split into thin rays, which reflect off the mirror board.

6 Darken the room. Move the torch until the light rays reflecting off the curved mirror are brought together at one spot, like radio waves on a dish antenna.

185

Listen to this

Sound is energy that moves back and forth through the air in the form of vibrations. These vibrations spread outward as waves, like the ripples caused by a stone when it is dropped into rather still water.

The first experiment demonstrates the existence and energy of sound waves. Channelling the sound inside a tube concentrates the waves in the direction of the tube. By channelling sound toward a candle, you can use the energy to blow out the flame.

The second experiment is all about the strength of sound waves. It shows that sounds get quieter if their waves are allowed to spread out. Scientists say that loud sounds have large amplitudes (variations of range).

In the final project, you can investigate pitch, or the range of sounds, by making a set of panpipes. Low sounds consist of a small number of vibrations every second. Musicians describe these sounds as having "low pitch" but scientists report the sounds as "low frequency." The panpipes show that pitch depends on the length of each pipe.

▲ **Play it again, Sam!**
You can play deep, low notes on a bass guitar. The sound waves vibrate slowly with a frequency as low as 50 times each second. High notes vibrate much more rapidly.

How sound travels

1 Stretch the food covering tightly over the end of the tube. Use the band to fasten it in place. You could also use a flat piece of rubber cut from a balloon instead of the food covering.

2 Ask an adult to light the candle. Point the tube at the candle, with the open end 10cm/4in from the flame. Give the food covering a sharp tap with the flat of your hand.

You will hear the sound coming out of the tube. It consists of pressure waves in the air. The tube concentrates the sound waves toward the candle flame and puts it out.

Sound waves

1 Place the watch close to your ear. You can hear a ticking sound coming from it. The sound becomes fainter when you move the watch away from your ear.

2 Place one end of the tube over a friend's ear, and hold the watch at the other end. The tube concentrates the sound and does not let it spread out. She can hear the watch clearly.

How to make panpipes

1 Cut the drinking straws so that you have four pairs that are 9cm/ 3½in, 8cm/3in, 7cm/2½in and 6cm/2in long. Block up one end of each straw with a small piece of modelling material.

2 Carefully cut out the card to the same shape as the blue piece shown above. Fix the straws into place with the tape from long to short, to align with card as shown.

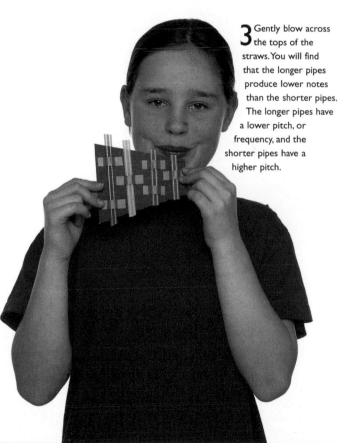

3 Gently blow across the tops of the straws. You will find that the longer pipes produce lower notes than the shorter pipes. The longer pipes have a lower pitch, or frequency, and the shorter pipes have a higher pitch.

Travel and Transportation

The most powerful, luxurious and specialized forms of transportation today all evolved from simple scientific principles. The trick of keeping a luxury passenger liner or a massive oil tanker afloat is basically the same as it was for early humans with their canoes and coracles. Many of the secrets of superpowered vehicles are the result of learning to make use of simple forces such as jet propulsion, thrust and lift, and combining them with other inventions and new materials. On the following pages, you will discover how boats, trains, cars, planes and spacecraft work by experimenting with the forces that make them go.

Simple boats

Some of the earliest and simplest types of boat are still made today. Small reed boats are still built in southern Iraq and on Lake Titicaca in South America in a similar way to the one in the project below. Reed boats are made by tying thousands of river reeds together into huge bundles. The bundles are then tied together to make hull shapes. In ancient Egypt, large boats were made like this, from papyrus reeds. Some historians believe that Egyptians may have made long ocean crossings in papyrus craft.

The model in the second project is of a coracle. This is a round boat made by covering a light wooden frame with animal hides. Coracles are also still made, but are now covered with canvas treated with tar instead of animal hide. Coracles were small enough for one person to paddle along a river and were used for fishing. When you are out near a river or lake, take photographs or make drawings of other simple craft, such as canoes and punts. See if you can make working models of them, too.

◀ **Afterlife evidence**
This boat was found in a pit alongside the Great Pyramid of Egypt in 1954. It is believed to have been used as a pharaoh's funeral boat, which ferried the dead pharaoh to the afterlife.

Make a reed craft

1 Make bundles of raffia by tying a few dozen strands together with a short piece of raffia. You will need two bundles about 20cm/8in long and two more about 25cm/10in long.

2 Tie the two long bundles and the two short bundles together. Tie the short bundles on top of the long ones. Fix a strand between each end, to make the ends bend up.

3 Gently lower the reed boat on to the surface of a tank of water. How well does it float? Does it stay upright? Try leaving it in the water to see if it becomes waterlogged.

Make a coracle

1 Cut one long piece of cane and three short pieces. Using short pieces of string, tie all three of the short pieces of cane to the long piece to make a triple-armed cross.

2 Cut a much longer piece of cane. Form it into a loop, and tie it to all the ends of the triple cross shape. Bend the ends of the cross up as you tie them to form a dish shape.

3 Cut pieces of cotton cloth about 15 x 5cm/6 x 2in. Apply glue to the outside of the frame, and place the pieces over it. Glue the pieces to each other where they overlap.

4 Glue down the cloth where it folds over the top of the frame. Put two coats of glue on the outside of the cloth to waterproof it. Leave the glue to dry completely.

When the model is dry, put the finished coracle into a tank of water. How well does it float? Why not try making a person from modelling material to sit in your model coracle?

Early Britons used coracles 9,000 years ago. Coracles are light to carry, easy to use, and stable enough to fish from.

Sail power

When you launch your model sailing boat, you can get an idea of how it is propelled by the wind. To sail in the direction they want to go, sailors must be aware of wind direction, so that they can adjust the position of the sails to make best use of it. If sailing boats face straight into the wind, the sails flap uselessly, and the boat is in a "no-go zone." They can, however, sail into oncoming wind by taking a zigzag course. This is called tacking. The wind blows against one side of the sail to propel the boat diagonally upwind. When the boat changes tack, the wind blows against the other side of the sail, and the boat goes forwards on the opposite diagonal. If the wind is blowing from behind the boat, the sail is set at right angles to the boat like an open wing, so that it is filled by the wind.

▲ **Parts of a sailboat**
Sailboats usually have a crew of two people. A helmsman operates the tiller and the mainsail, and a crew who works the jib and centreboard (which stops the boat from drifting sideways).

Template ▶

YOU WILL NEED

pencil, ruler, cardboard, scissors, adhesive tape, plastic sheet, stapler, bradawl, non-hardening modelling material, thin garden canes, coloured paper, plastic straw, small plastic bottle, string, paper clip, sheet of paper.

Make a sailboat

1 Cut out your hull shape from thick cardboard, using the template above as a guide. Score along the dotted lines with the scissors. Use adhesive tape to fasten the sides together.

2 Lay the hull on a plastic sheet. Cut the plastic around the hull, allowing enough to cover the sides and overlap at the top by 5cm/2in. Fold the sheet over the hull and staple it in place.

3 Make a hole in the middle of a strip of cardboard a little wider than the hull. Staple in place. Put modelling material under the hole, and push a 30cm/12in cane through the hole into it.

4 Cut a sail from coloured paper with a base of about 20cm/8in. Attach the straw along the side and a garden cane along the bottom with tape. Slip the straw over the mast.

5 Cut an L-shape (about 8cm/3in long, 4cm/1½in wide at the base and 2cm/¾in wide at the top) from the small plastic bottle. Cut the base of the L in half to make two slanted tabs.

6 Fold back the two tabs of the L-shaped plastic in opposite directions, as shown, and staple them to the stern (back) of the boat. This is the boat's rudder.

7 Cut a piece of string about 20cm/8in long. Tape one end to the back of the boom (the cane), and feed the other end through a paper clip attached to the back of the boat.

8 To test out how your sail boat works, make a breeze by waving a large sheet of paper near to the boat. Adjust the string to move the sail into the right position.

When you have finished your boat, you could try making and adding a centreboard. Attach a cardboard oblong at right angles to the bottom of the boat. It will stop your boat from drifting sideways in the wind.

direction of wind

When you test your boat, set the sail in these different positions. Alter the position of the sail by using the string taped to the boom (cane). Follow the arrows shown here to see which way the wind should be blowing from in each case. Try blowing from other directions to see if this makes a difference to your boat.

How ships float

The simplest boats, such as rafts, float because the material they are made of is less dense (lighter) than water. Heavy ships can float, because the water they are floating in pushes upwards against them. This pushing force is called upthrust. The first experiment shows that an object will float if the upthrust of the water is great enough to overcome the downward push of the object's weight. The size of the upthrust depends on how much water the object pushes out of the way. When you put an object in water and let it go, it settles into the water, pushing liquid out of the way. The farther it goes in, the more water it pushes away and the more upthrust acts on it. When the upthrust becomes the same as the object's weight, the object floats.

The second project shows you a hollow hull. If you push a light, hollow ball under water, it will spring back up. Upthrust from the water makes a hollow hull float in the same way. The higher the density of water, the greater the upthrust. This means that ships float slightly higher in salt water, since it is more dense than fresh water.

salt water

fresh water

▲ Measuring density

The density of water is measured with a hydrometer. You can make one by putting a lump of modelling material on the end of a straw. Put it in a glass of water, and mark the water level with tape. Now put the straw in an equal amount of salty water. What happens?

Testing upthrust

1 Put the two styrofoam chunks into a large tank of water. They will float well, because their material is so light. Only a small amount of upthrust is needed.

2 Try pushing the chunks under the water. Now you are pushing lots of water aside. Can you feel upthrust pushing back? The bigger chunk will experience more upthrust.

3 A wooden block floats deeper in the water, because wood is more dense (heavier) than styrofoam. A marble sinks, because the upthrust on it is not as great as its weight.

Hollow hulls

1 Put a piece of foil about 20 x 15cm/ 8 x 6in into a tank of water. With just the slightest push, it will sink. This is because it does not displace much water, so there is very little upthrust.

2 Lift the sheet of foil out of the water, and dry it carefully with a paper towel. Now form it into a simple boat shape with your fingers. Take care not to tear the foil.

3 Put your foil boat into the water. It should now float. It will not sink so easily. Its shape pushes aside much more water than it did when it was flat, so the upthrust is greater.

Try filling your foil boat with small objects, such as marbles, for cargo. As you put more marbles in, it will float lower and lower. How many marbles can your boat hold before it sinks?

This simple foil boat works like a real ship's hull. Even though it is made of metal, it is filled with air. This gives the hull shape a much lower overall density.

What's in a hull?

Whenever an object such as a ship moves through the water, the water slows it down. The push made by the water is called water resistance, or drag. The faster the object moves, the greater the water resistance becomes.

If you look around a busy port, you will see dozens of different hull designs. Sleek, narrow hulls with sharp bows cause less resistance than wide hulls with square bows, so they can move through the water faster.

You can test how the shape of a bow affects the speed of a ship in this experiment. The deeper a hull sits in the water, the more resistance there is. Some hulls are designed to sit just on top of the water. For example, a small speedboat has a flaring, shallow V-shaped hull designed to skim across the surface. A cargo ship has a square hull that sits lower in the water. Speed is not as important for the cargo ship as it is for the speedboat. Instead, the cargo ship is designed for stability, and to carry as much as possible.

Testing hull shapes

1 Use a ruler to draw the three templates shown left on sheets of stiff cardboard. Make sure the corners are square and the edges straight. Carefully cut out the shapes.

2 Using scissors, score along the lines inside the base of the square boat (shown as dotted lines left). Bend up the sides, and use adhesive tape to fix the corners together.

3cm/1¼in

3cm/1¼in

15cm/6in

15cm/6in

3cm/1¼in

15cm/6in

15cm/6in

3cm/1¼in

10cm/4in

3cm/1¼in

15cm/6in

10cm/4in

▲ Templates

Use these three templates to help you cut out and make the three boat shapes in this project.

3 Make the round-ended and pointed boats in the same way as the first boat. Use a separate piece of cardboard to make the round bow, and tape it to the base in several places.

4 Now cover the outside of each shape with foil, neatly folding the foil over the sides. This will make the shapes more waterproof. Fix a paper clip to the bow (front) of each boat.

5 Roll out three balls of modelling material about the size of a walnut. Weigh the balls to make sure they are the same weight. Attach a ball to the bow of each boat with string.

6 Put a large plastic bowl on a table or a strong box. Use a watering can to pour water into the trough. The water should be about 1cm/½in from the top of the bowl.

Release the boats all at the same time. The weighted strings will pull them along down the length of the bowl. Which one wins the race to the other end of the bowl? Try timing the boats with a stopwatch to work out the difference between the fastest and slowest.

7 Line up the boats at one end of the bowl. Hang the strings and modelling material balls down over the other end. Put a small wooden brick inside each boat.

Power and steering afloat

The model boat in this project is fitted with two basic devices for controlling water craft. Both operate underwater. The propeller is driven by the engine of a motor- or steam-powered boat. It rotates very fast and pushes the craft through the water. In the project, the engine power comes from the energy stored in a wound-up rubber band. As in real life propellers, the blades are set at different angles, and push the water backwards, so thrusting the vessel forwards, as it spins. You could try making different propeller designs – with more blades set at different angles, for example – and testing them to see which works best.

A rudder is used to steer both sail- and motor-powered boats. It is controlled by a handle called a tiller, or a wheel, on the boat. As in your model boat, the rudder can be moved to different positions to make the boat turn left or right, but will only work when the boat is actually moving. In addition to making the boat turn left and right, the rudder also keeps the boat going in a straight line when it is set straight.

▲ Making a connection
In a large cruise yacht, the rudder is moved by wires linked to the wheel in the cockpit. The wheel drives the sprocket, which moves a chain. Wires attached to the chain move the rudder via pulleys. The yacht is also equipped with a diesel engine that is connected to a single propeller via a driveshaft.

YOU WILL NEED

cork, bradawl, scissors, small plastic bottle, large plastic bottle, large paper clip, pliers (optional), ruler, bead, long rubber bands, small pencil, pool, thin garden cane.

Make a powered boat

1 Make a hole through the middle of the cork using a bradawl. Cut a diagonal slot in either side of the cork. Push two strips of plastic cut from a small bottle into the slots.

2 Cut an oblong strip from one side of the large plastic bottle. This slot is the top of your boat. With the bradawl, make a small hole at the back of your bottle in the bottom.

3 Straighten a large paper clip (you may need pliers). Bend the last 1.5cm/½in of wire at right angles. Push the wire through the cork, and thread it through the bead and small hole.

4 Bend the end of the wire inside the bottle. Hook a rubber band over the wire, and stretch it up through the neck of the bottle. Secure it in place with a pencil.

5 To wind up the band, turn the pencil as you hold on to the propeller. Keep holding the propeller until you put the boat into the water and release it. What happens?

6 Now make a rudder for your boat. Cut a piece of plastic about 4 x 4cm/1½ x 1½in and pierce two holes near one edge. Push a piece of thin cane through the two holes.

7 Use the strip of plastic cut from the large bottle to support your rudder. Pierce two holes about 2cm/¾in apart in the middle of the strip, and push the cane through them.

8 Fix the rudder support to the bottle with a rubber band, so that the rudder is clear of the propeller. Wind up the pencil, and put your boat back in the water.

Like a real boat builder, you will want to test the controls of your boat. To do this, start with the rudder in the middle to make the boat go straight. Next, try turning the rudder from side to side. What happens? How tight a circle can you make your boat turn in?

rubber band engine   propeller   rudder

Safety at sea

There are various ways in which ships can be designed to keep afloat. All ships have bilge pumps that pump out water that has collected in the bottom of the hull and expel it into the sea or river. Many sailboats and canoes are fitted with bags of air or styrofoam bricks inside to keep them buoyant (afloat). Most lifeboats are self-righting, which means that they bob back upright if they capsize, like the model in the first project. Self-righting lifeboats are completely watertight – even the air inlets in inflatable lifeboats have seals to keep out water. Heavy engines are set low down and the hull and high cabins are full of air. This arrangement makes the lifeboat flip upright automatically.

The second and third projects show how hydrofoils and hovercrafts work. These are fast boats, designed for short sea crossings. A hydrofoil is the fastest type of ferry. Under the hull, there are winglike foils. Water flows faster over the foil's curved upper surface than it does over the flat lower surface, creating lift. When going at high speed, the foils lift the hull clear of the water.

Try the third project to see how hovercrafts skim across the water supported on cushions of air. Buoyancy tanks stop the hovercraft from sinking if the air cushion fails.

Self-righting boat

1 Cut a boat shape about 15 x 10cm/ 6 x 4in from styrofoam. Attach a golf-ball sized lump of modelling material to one side of your boat shape with a rubber band.

2 Put your boat into a tank or bowl of water. Have the modelling material, which represents the crew and equipment, on top. If you capsize the boat, it will stay capsized.

3 Add another lump of modelling material underneath the boat, to represent heavy engines or ballast. Add an upturned plastic tub on top to represent a watertight cabin.

4 Now try to capsize it again, and it will flip back upright. This is because the air, trapped underwater by the tub and a heavy weight on top, forces the boat upright again.

How a hydrofoil works

I Cut a rectangle of plastic, about 5 x 10cm/2 x 4in, from the lid of the margarine container. Fold it in half. Staple the ends together 1cm/½in in from the back edge.

2 Use a bradawl to make a hole in the front of the hydrofoil 1cm/½in away from the folded edge. Use pliers to bend 1.5cm/¾in of one end of the wire. Slide the hydrofoil on to the wire.

3 Make sure the hydrofoil moves freely on the wire. Move your hydrofoil in air – it will not lift up, because air is far less dense than water. Pull it through water, and it will rise up the wire.

How a hovercraft works

YOU WILL NEED

How a hydrofoil works:

margarine tub lid, ruler, scissors, stapler, bradawl, pliers, coat hanger wire (ask an adult to cut it), tank or bowl of water.

How a hovercraft works: ruler, styrofoam tray, pencil, balloon, balloon pump, button.

I Use a ruler to find the middle of the styrofoam tray. Poke a hole through the middle with the pointed end of a pencil. The hole should be about 1cm/½in across.

2 Blow up the balloon with the pump, and carefully push its neck through the hole. Keep pinching the neck of the balloon to stop the air from escaping.

3 Keep pinching the neck of the balloon with one hand, using the other hand to slip the button into the neck. The button will control how fast the air escapes.

4 Place the tray on a table. Air escapes steadily from under the tray's edges, lifting it up a tiny bit. Give the tray a gentle push, and it will skate over the surface.

Submarine action

tanks are full of air and valves are closed.

valves open and tanks fill with water.

tanks full – submarine submerged.

air is forced in, so water is forced out

A submarine dives by making itself heavier so that it sinks. It surfaces again by making itself lighter. Submarines use large tanks called buoyancy tanks. When the submarine is on the surface, these tanks are full of air. To make the submarine dive, the tanks are flooded with seawater, making the submarine heavy enough to sink. To make the submarine surface again, compressed air is pumped into the tanks, forcing the water out. This makes the submarine lighter, and it floats to the surface. When submarines are underwater, they move up and down using tiny wings called hydroplanes. These work like rudders to control the submarine's direction. Submarines need very strong hulls to prevent them from being crushed by the huge pressure under the water. As submarines dive, the weight of the water pressing down on them becomes greater and greater. You can see how this works by making this model.

> ### YOU WILL NEED
> large plastic bottle, sand, plastic funnel, tank of water, two small plastic bottles, bradawl, scissors, ruler, two plastic drinking straws, rubber bands, non-hardening modelling material, two bulldog clips.

Make a submarine

1 Fill the large plastic bottle with sand using a funnel. Fill it until it just sinks in a tank of water. Test the bottle (cap firmly screwed on) to find the right amount of sand.

2 With adult help, make a large hole (about 1cm/½in across) in one side of two small plastic bottles. On the other side make a small hole, big enough for a plastic straw to fit into.

3 Attach the two small bottles to both sides of the large bottle using rubber bands. Twist the small bottles so that the small hole on each one points upwards.

4 Push a plastic straw into each small hole, so that a bit pokes through. Seal around the base of the straws with modelling material to make a watertight joint.

5 Put a small bulldog clip about halfway down each straw. The clips need to be strong enough to squash the straw and stop air from being forced out by the water.

This is the finished model submarine. You might find that your model sinks bow (front) first, or stern (back) first. If this is the case, level it by shaking the sand evenly inside the bottle.

6 Put your model submarine in a tank of water. With the clips on, it should float. Remove the clips and water will flood the buoyancy tanks. The submarine will sink.

7 To make the submarine surface again, blow slowly into both straws at once. The air will force the water out of the buoyancy tanks, and the submarine will rise to the surface.

8 When your model submarine has resurfaced, keep blowing slowly into the tanks. Replace each bulldog clip and your model submarine will remain floating on the surface.

▲ Parts of a submarine

A modern submarine, such as this nuclear ballistic missile submarine, is almost as long as a football field – 91m/100yd. It has an engine and propeller at the stern, and is operated by a crew of 140. Steam drives the turbines that turn the propeller. A submarine's hull is strong, but few submarines can go below 500m/1,600ft.

Making rails

A full freight or passenger train is heavy, so the track it runs on has to be tough. Nowadays, rails are made from steel, which is a much stronger material than the cast iron used for the first railways. The shape of the rail also helps to make it strong. If you sliced through a rail from top to bottom, you would see it has an "I"-shaped cross section. The broad, flat bottom narrows into the "waist" of the I, and widens again into a curved head. Most countries use a rail shaped like this.

Tracks are made up of pieces of rail, which are laid on wooden or concrete crossbeams called sleepers. Train wheels are a set distance apart, so rails must be a set distance apart, too. The distance between rails is called the gauge. This project will show you how to make sets of railway tracks for the models on the following pages. Make at least two sets of tracks – the more tracks you make, the farther your train can travel.

<table>
<tr><td>YOU WILL NEED</td></tr>
<tr><td>two sheets of cardboard measuring 26 x 11cm/10¼ x 4¼in, pencil, ruler, scissors, white glue and glue brush, silver and brown paint, paintbrush, water pot, one sheet of foam board measuring 13 x 20cm/5 x 8in one sheet of A4 paper, masking tape, one sheet of thin card measuring 10 x 5cm/4 x 2in.</td></tr>
</table>

rodding cables from points signal box

direction of train

guard rails guide wheels and avoid derailment

points

points are moved by an electric motor

◀ Points system

Trains are switched from one track to another using points. Part of the track (the blade) moves to guide the wheels smoothly from one route to another. A signaller moves the blades by pulling a lever in the signal box. The blade and the lever are connected by metal rods. The lever cannot be pulled unless the signal is clear.

Making tracks

1 Place one 26 x 11cm/10¼in x 4¼in piece of card lengthways. Draw a line 1cm/½in in from each of the outside edges. Draw two more lines, 3.5cm/2¼in in from the outside edges. This is side A.

2 Turn the cardboard over (side B) and place it lengthways. Draw lines 4cm/1½in and 4.75cm/1¾in in from each edge. Repeat steps 1 and 2 with the second piece of 26 x 11cm/10¼in x 4¼in card.

3 Hold the ruler firmly against one of the lines you have drawn. Use the tip of a pair of scissors to score along the line. Repeat for all lines on both sides of both pieces of cardboard.

4 Place the cards A side up. For each piece in turn, fold firmly along the two lines. Fold up from the scored side. Turn the card over. Repeat for the lines on side B.

5 With the A side up, press the folds into the I-shape of the rail. Open out again. Glue the B side of the 2cm/¾in wide middle section as shown. Repeat for the second rail.

6 Give your two rails a metallic look by painting the upper (A) sides silver. Leave the paint to dry, and then apply a second coat. Leave the second coat to dry.

7 Use a pencil and ruler to mark ten 13 x 2cm/5 x ¾in strips on the foam board. Cut them out. Glue two strips together to make five thick railway sleepers. Leave them to dry.

8 Paint the sleepers brown on their tops and sides, to make them look like wood. Leave them to dry, then apply a second coat of paint. Leave the second coat to dry, too.

9 Lay the sleepers on the piece of paper, 3cm/1¼in apart. Make sure that they are exactly parallel to each other. Run a strip of masking tape down the middle to hold them in place.

10 Glue the base of a rail, and press into place with the outside edge of the rail 1.5cm/¾in in from the edge of the sleeper. Repeat with the other track. Secure with masking tape until it is dry.

Make several sets of rails. To join the rails together, roll up the thin card. Insert one end into the top of the I-shape. Push the second rail into the other end.

Rolling stock

The vehicle and machinery that is carried by a modern locomotive's underframe and wheels may weigh up to 100 tons. As bigger and more powerful locomotives were built, more wheels were added to carry the extra weight. Early steam locomotives had only two pairs of wheels. Later steam locomotives had two, three or four pairs of driving wheels, one pair of which was directly driven from the cylinders. The cylinders house the pistons, whose movement pushes the driving wheels around via a connecting rod.

The other wheels are connected to the driving wheel by a coupling rod, so that they turn at the same time. The small wheels in front of the driving wheels are called leading wheels. The ones behind are the trailing wheels. Locomotives are defined by the total number of wheels they have. For example, a 4-4-0 type locomotive has four leading, four driving and no trailing wheels. This project shows you how to make an underframe for a 4-4-0 type locomotive, which will run on the tracks described on the previous page. The following page shows how to make a locomotive to sit on the underframe.

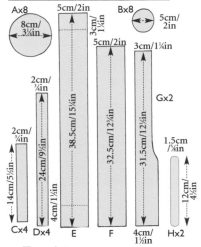

YOU WILL NEED

large sheet of cardboard, pencil, ruler, pair of compasses, scissors, white glue and glue brush, masking tape, four 10cm/4in lengths of 0.5cm/¼in diameter dowel, four pieces of 5 x 5cm/2 x 2in thin card, silver and black paint, paintbrush, water pot, four map pins.

▲ **Templates**
Draw and cut out the templates from the cardboard. Use a pair of compasses to draw the wheel templates A and B.

Make an underframe

1 Roll the rim templates C and D into rings. Glue and tape to hold. Glue each small wheel circle to each side of a small ring as shown. Repeat for the big wheels. Leave to dry.

2 Use a pencil to enlarge the compass hole on one side of each wheel. Glue one end of each piece of dowel. Push them into the holes of two big and two small wheels.

3 Roll the 5 x 5cm/2 x 2in card into sleeves to fit loosely over each piece of dowel. Tape to hold. Make wheel pairs by fixing the remaining wheels to the dowel as described in step 2.

4 When the glue is dry, paint all four pairs of wheels silver. You do not need to paint the dowel axles. Paint two coats, letting the first dry before you apply the second.

5 Use a ruler and pencil to mark eight equal segments on the outside of each wheel. Paint a small circle over the compass hole, and the middle of each segment black.

6 Fold along the dotted lines on E. Glue all three straight edges of template G and stick to template E. Repeat this for the other side. Secure all joints with masking tape.

7 Glue the open edges of the underframe. Fit template F on top and hold until firm. Tape over the joints. Give the underframe two coats of black paint. Leave to dry.

8 Glue the card sleeves to the base of the underframe. Small wheel axles go 3cm/1¼in and 7cm/2¾in from the front, big wheels 3.5cm/1¼in and 13cm/5in from the back. Tape to secure.

9 Paint the coupling rods (H) with a coat of silver paint. Allow the paint to dry thoroughly. Then give the coupling rods a second coat of paint, and leave them to dry.

10 Press a map pin through each end of the coupling rods, about 0.5cm/¼in from the edge. Carefully press the pin into each big wheel about 1.5cm/⅝in beneath the middle.

The wheels of the underframe will fit on the model tracks just like those of a real train. In real trains, however, the wheels are mounted in swivelling units called "bogies."

Brake van

Few early steam locomotives had brakes. If the driver needed to stop quickly, he had to throw the engine into reverse. By the early 1860s, braking systems for steam locomotives had been invented. Some passenger carriages also had their own handbrakes that were operated by the carriage guards. A brake van was added to the back of trains, too, but its brakes were operated by a guard riding inside. Old-style brake vans, like the one in this project, sat at the end of the train, so that the guard could make sure that all the carriages stayed coupled.

The problem was that the train driver had no control over the rest of the train. When he wanted to stop, he had to blow the engine whistle to warn each of the carriage guards to apply their brakes. The brakes on a locomotive and its carriages or wagons needed to be linked. This was made possible by the invention of an air-braking system in 1869. When the driver applies the brakes, compressed air travels along pipes that link all the train, and presses brake shoes. Air brakes are now used on nearly all the world's railroads.

YOU WILL NEED

large piece of cardboard, small piece of thin red card for template J, ruler, pencil, scissors, white glue and brush, masking tape, four 10cm/4in lengths of 5mm/¼in-diameter dowel, acrylic paints, brush, pot, two 3cm/1¼in lengths of 5mm/¼in-diameter dowel, pair of compasses.

▲ **Templates**

Make a brake van

1 Copy the templates on to cardboard and cut them out. Glue templates A, B, and C together to make the underframe as shown. Tape over the joints to secure them.

2 Make and paint two pairs of small wheels (2in diameter) following steps 1 through 3 in the "Underframe" project on p208. Glue and tape the wheel pairs to the underframe.

3 Glue the bottom edges of the van sides (E) to the van base (D). Then glue on the van ends (F). Secure the joints with masking tape until the glue is dry.

4 Paint the brake van brown with black details, and the wheels and underframe black and silver. Apply two coats of paint, letting each one dry between coats.

5 Paint one side of template G black. Let the paint dry before applying a second coat. Glue the top edges of the van. Bend the roof to fit on the top of the van, as shown.

6 Apply glue to the top surface of the underframe. Stick the brake van centrally on top. Press it together until the glue holds firm. Leave the model to dry completely.

7 Roll up templates I into two 2cm/ ¾in tubes to fit loosely over the 3cm/ 1¼in pieces of dowel. Tape to hold. Paint them silver. Paint the buffer templates H black and stick on each dowel.

8 Use compasses to pierce two holes 2.5cm/1in from each side of the van and 1.5cm/⅝in up. Enlarge with a pencil. Glue the end of each dowel buffer. Slot it into the hole. Leave to dry.

9 Cut a 2cm/¾in slot between the buffers. Fold the red card template J in half. Glue each open end of the loop, and push them through the slot. Press down to hold firm.

The brake van will also run on the tracks you made in the "Making tracks" project on p206. You can also join the red-card coupling to join the brake van to the model locomotive you made in the "Toy train" project on p210. On old-style railways, the brake van had one of two brake systems. One had hand-operated brakes that worked on the tread of the brake van's wheels. The other had a valve that allowed the guard to apply air brakes to all of the vehicles in the train.

Making car wheels turn

cylinder head

spark plug

cylinder

piston

con
(connecting) rod

crankshaft

This experiment shows how one kind of movement – that goes around and around – can be converted into an up-and-down movement. This idea is applied to cars to make the wheels go around, but it happens the other way around. The up-and-down movement of the pistons is changed into the circular motion of the crankshaft and wheels. When a car engine is switched on, fuel ignites and hot gases are produced in the cylinders. The gases force close-fitting pistons down the cylinders in which they are housed. The pistons are connected to the crankshaft (a rod that connects eventually to the wheels), so that as they move up and down, the crankshaft rotates. This, in turn, makes the wheels go around. One up-and-down movement of a piston results in one turn of the crankshaft. The wheels rotate once for about every three to six turns of the crankshaft.

▲ Working together

Most car engines have four cylinders arranged like this. You can see the pistons and cylinders. Four rods, one from each piston, turn metal joints attached to the crankshaft. As the rods turn the joints, the crankshaft moves around. This movement is transmitted to the wheels, via the gearbox, which controls how fast the wheels turn relative to the engine.

Changing motion

1 Place the shoebox narrow-side-down on a flat surface. With one hand, push the metal rod through the middle, making sure that your other hand will not get jabbed by the rod.

2 Using the pliers, bend the rod at right angles where it comes out of the box. Attach the jar lid to it with tape. Push the lid until it rests against the side of the box.

3 Carefully use the pliers to bend the piece of rod sticking out of the other side of the box. This will make a handle for the piston, so that you will be able to turn it easily.

4 Cut a piece of thick plastic straw about 5cm/2in long, and tape it to the side of the box close to the jar lid. Make sure that it just sticks up beyond the edge of the box.

5 Draw a design in pencil on a piece of stiff paper. Copy the jester shown in this project, or draw a simple clown. Choose something that looks good when it moves.

6 Using the felt-tipped pens, shade the design until it looks the way you want it to. The more vivid the figure is, the nicer it will look on the top of the piston.

7 Carefully cut the finished drawing out of the paper. Make sure that you have a clean-edged design. Try not to smudge the felt-tipped pen with your fingers.

8 Turn the drawing over. Use the tape to attach the thin plastic straw to the bottom of the drawing. About 2cm/¾in of straw should be attached.

Place the box on end so the jester is at the top. Turn the handle on the front. As you turn the handle, the jar lid revolves and pushes the jester up and down, like a piston.

9 Slide the straw attached to the drawing into the straw taped to the box. It will come out of the other end. Push down so that the straw touches the edge of the jar lid.

Changing gear

Gears in a car help transfer movement in the most efficient way. They do this by transmitting movement from the crankshaft (which links engine and wheels) to another shaft called the propeller shaft. The propeller shaft rotates more slowly than the crankshaft and adapts the movement, so that the car can cope better with different speeds and efforts, such as starting and going uphill. The change in speed of rotation between the two shafts is controlled from the car's gearbox. As a driver changes gear, toothed wheels that are connected to the crankshaft engage with other toothed wheels joined to the propeller shaft. The difference in the number of teeth on each wheel determines the number of times the wheels turn, as the first project demonstrates. The second experiment shows how gear wheels work in a car. The larger corrugated cardboard wheel has more teeth than the two smaller wheels.

crankshaft

propeller shaft

high gear low gear

▲ Wheels within wheels
The car's engine turns the crankshaft with different-sized gears (toothed wheels) on it. High gears are used for more speed, because the big wheel turns the small wheel faster. The gear system is called the transmission – it transmits (moves) the engine's power to the car's wheels. Most cars have five gears. The biggest is needed for slow speeds, and the smallest for high speeds.

YOU WILL NEED

pair of compasses, ruler, pencil, A4 sheet of white paper, black pen, scissors, A4 sheet of thin card, two strips of corrugated cardboard, adhesive tape, three different felt-tipped pens.

Drawing the gears

1 Using the compasses, trace a 14cm/5½in-diameter circle on the paper. Draw over it with the pen and cut it out. On the card, trace, draw, and cut out an 11cm/4¼in-diameter circle.

2 Tape corrugated card around the circles. Make a hole in the small circle wide enough for the tip of a felt-tipped pen. Turn the small wheel inside the larger. Trace the path in felt-tipped pen.

3 Make a second hole in the small wheel. Turn the small gear inside the larger using another felt-tipped pen. Make a third hole in the small wheel and use a third felt-tipped pen.

Three-gear machine

1 Use the compasses to trace one 14cm/5½in-diameter and two 11cm/4¼in-diameter circles on the cardboard. Draw around the edges with the pen, and cut the circles out.

2 Carefully wrap the strips of corrugated cardboard around the circles, using one strip per circle, corrugated side out. Tape each strip to the bottom of the circles.

As you turn the gears, notice how they move in opposite directions to each other. Now you have a three-gear machine, where the energy from each gear is being transferred to the others, just like the gears in a car.

3 Place the largest gear wheel on the piece of fibreboard. Hold the gear down and glue the dowel on to the side of the gear base at the edge of the wheel. Leave it until it is dry.

4 Position all three gears on the fibreboard, with the edges just touching each other. Pin each of them firmly to the fibreboard with a map pin, but allow them to turn.

5 Gently turn the dowel on the largest gear. As that gear turns, the two others that are linked together by the corrugated card will turn against it.

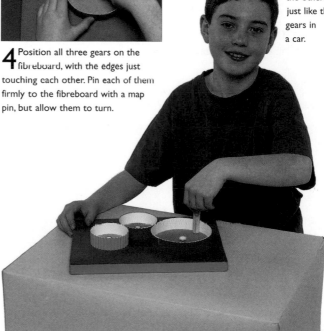

Car control

Cars have two kinds of brakes. Parking brakes lock the rear wheels when the car is standing still. Disc brakes slow down the car when it is moving, in the same way that the sandpaper slows the model wheel in the first experiment.

The second project shows how a device called the camshaft controls the flow of fuel into the cylinders. The camshaft is designed so as to have a regular action that opens one valve and closes another at the same time. Inlet valves let fuel and air into the engine, and burned waste gases are removed via the outlet valves. The camshaft controls make the engine run smoothly.

filtered air

gasoline

fuel and air mixture

▲ The carburettor

Fuel and air enter the carburettor in just the right quantities for the car to run smoothly. The mixture is then fed into the cylinders. Pressing the accelerator pedal in a car allows more air and fuel into the engine to make it run faster, so speeding up the car.

Stopping ▶

When a driver presses the brake pedal, a piston presses together two pads, one on either side of the disc to which the wheel is attached. This strong grip stops the disc from turning, and as the disc slows, so do the wheels.

piston

disc

wheel attached here

calliper

brake pads

Disc brakes

1 Use the scissors to cut a narrow 40cm/16in strip from the fabric. You may have to use special fabric cutting scissors if your ordinary scissors are not sharp enough.

2 Take the strip of fabric you have cut out and wrap it around the rim of the circular cardboard box. Secure it firmly in place with small pieces of tape.

3 Make a hole in the middle of the box's lid with a pencil. Twist the pencil until it comes through the base of the box. Now gently push the wood dowel through both holes.

4 Spread lots of glue on to the sandpaper's smooth side. Wrap the sandpaper carefully over the top of the wood block. Pressing firmly, stick it together. Leave it to dry.

5 Stand two plastic cups upside down. Rest either end of the dowel on each cup. Cut two small pieces of insulation tape. Use them to fix each end of the dowel to the cup bases.

6 Spin the lid fast on the dowel. As it spins, bring the sandpaper into contact with the edge of the lid. Test the brake disc to see how quickly you can stop the lid.

How valves work

1 Use scissors to cut a 1 x 12cm/ ½ x 4½in strip from the cardboard. Double it over in the middle. Hold it with your fingertips. Bend the two ends of the card away from one another.

2 Cut a 1 x 4cm/½ x 1½in strip from the original piece of card. Use masking tape to fix the card strip to the bent bottom ends of the first piece. This makes a triangle shape.

3 Use the scissors to cut out two small circle shapes from the original piece of card. Use masking tape to secure them to the bottom piece of the triangle you have made.

4 Put the cardboard triangle on top of the cardboard tube. The circles should touch the plastic lid. With a pencil, mark the position where the circles sit on the lid.

5 Using the scissors, carefully cut around the pencil marks you have made in the plastic lid of the tube. These form an inlet and an outlet. As one valve opens, the other will close.

6 Now you can rock the triangle back and forth, to cover and uncover the two holes. This is just how a camshaft opens and shuts the inlet and outlet valves in a car's cylinder.

Keeping cool

The explosion of fuel and air that fires a car's engine generates a great deal of heat. Friction (rubbing together of two surfaces), as the engine parts move together at speed, also creates heat. If the heat level is not kept down, the engine stops working. Metal parts expand, seize up and stop. To cool the engine, water from the car's radiator is pumped around the hottest parts of the engine – the combustion chambers, where the fuel ignites, and the cylinders.

▲ **Mass production**
All the separate parts of a car are mass-produced and then assembled (put together) on a production line to make the finished vehicle. Almost all cars are assembled on production lines today. Robots do much of the work.

The moving water carries heat away from the hottest parts of the engine. The radiator cools the hot water from the engine by using a fan. The fan is driven by a belt connected to the engine. This project shows how a belt transfers turning movement from one shaft to another. This is how a car's engine turns the fan belt.

Fan belt

1 Using the ruler, measure five 2.5cm/1in-wide strips on the thin cloth. The height of the reels of thread should be more than 2.5cm/1in. Use the scissors to cut out each strip.

2 Wrap one of the fabric strips around each of the five reels of thread. Glue each strip at the end, so that it sits firmly around the reel and will not come loose.

3 Place the reels on the wooden board as shown above. Trace the outlines with a pencil. Put the nails through the middle of the reels and carefully hammer them into the board.

4 Wind the ribbon around the reels, with the velvet side against four of the reels. Cut the ribbon at the point where you can join both ends around the fifth reel.

5 Tape the two ends of the ribbon together. Make sure that the ribbon wraps firmly around all of the five reels, but not so tightly that it can't move.

6 Use the compasses to draw circles about 7cm/1¾in in diameter on to the five pieces of card. Then carefully draw freehand spiral shapes inside each circle.

7 Use the scissors to cut each spiral out of each of the pieces of card. Start from the outside edge, and gradually work your way in along the lines of the spiral.

8 Tape one end of each spiral to the end of a skewer. Wind the other end of the spiral around the skewer stick a few times. Tape it close to the opposite end of the skewer.

Now you are ready to turn the belt. Like a fan belt in a car, it turns the fans around. This is a five-fan machine. You can add more fans if you like.

9 Put a small amount of tape on to the end of each wooden skewer. Then place each skewer into one of the empty holes in the top of each reel of thread.

Prototype car

When you make your model car, choose the paint carefully. Do you want bright tones that will be noticed, or cool, fashionable shades? Car manufacturers call in teams of people to help them decide what a car should look like. Stylists and design and production engineers join forces with the sales team to develop cars they hope people will buy. They think about the paint, how much people are prepared to pay, and what features they want, from air-conditioning to special car seats.

Before a new car is launched to the public, detailed models are made and tested to investigate the car's aerodynamics (how air flows over its shape). Finally, a prototype (early version) of the car is built and tested for road handling, engine quality and comfort.

Wire basket ▸
Car designers today make use of CAD (computer-aided design) software to help them create a three-dimensional image of a new car design. Wire-frame (see-through) computer images show the car from any angle. They also show how all the parts of the car fit together.

Model car

1 Draw and cut out four 2.5cm/1in and eight 6cm/2½in diameter cardboard circles. Glue the 6cm/2½in circles to make four wheels. Glue a 2.5cm/1in circle to the middle of each wheel.

2 Use the bradawl to make a hole in the middle of each wheel. Cut four 4mm/⅛in strips of coloured card. Wrap one each around the wheel rims. Glue the overlapping ends.

3 Push straightened paper clips into the holes and bend the outer ends with pliers. Fix the wheels to the two pieces of dowel by pushing the paper clips into the ends.

4 Cut a piece of 8 x 15cm/2¾ x 6in cardboard. Trim one end to make it 6cm/2½in wide. Tape the axles to the card, one at each end. Make sure they are long enough for the wheels to rotate freely.

5 Cut a piece of cardboard 8 x 35cm/ 3¼ x 14in. Double it over and bend it into a British cab shape. Tape the two loose ends together. Stick the base of the cab shape to the car base.

6 Cut two cardboard shapes 15cm/6in long and 10cm/4in high. Trim them with the scissors to the same shape as the side of your car cab. Attach the sides to the cab with tape.

Decorate your car

1 Remove the wheels from your car. Paint the sides and top of the cab with one of the two shades of paint. Leave it to dry. Then paint it with the same shade again, and leave it to dry.

2 Draw exciting designs for the sides of the car and a driver to go behind the windscreen. Draw some head lamps and some exhaust fumes. Add patterns with the felt-tipped pens.

Replace the wheels when they are dry. Now your car looks just like a real vehicle. Cut photographs of cars from magazines to get ideas for new designs.

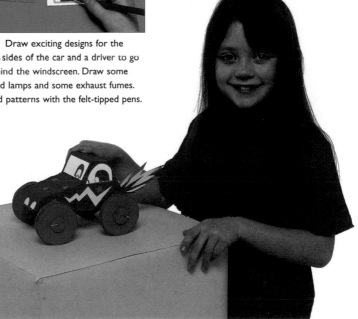

3 Let the paint dry for a couple of hours. Cut the designs out of the card. Glue them to the sides and back of the car. Paint the wheels with the shade of paint you haven't used.

Parachutes and balloons

Parachutes fall slowly because air is trapped beneath them. They are deliberately designed to have very high drag. Drag is the force that works against the direction of anything that flies through the air. The amount of drag depends on the shape. A fat, lumpy shape, such as the parachute in the first project, has lots of drag and falls slowly.

Hot air balloons rise into the air, because the hot air inside them is lighter than the air outside. Real balloons use gas burners, but the project here uses a hair dryer to make the balloon rise.

Mini-parachute jump

1 Use the felt-tipped pen to draw around the plate on the fabric. Using the scissors, carefully cut out the circle to make what will be the parachute's canopy.

2 Make about eight equally spaced marks around the edge of the circle. Use a needle to sew on one 30cm/12in long piece of thread to each point you have marked.

3 Use tape to secure the free end of each thread to a reel. Use a plastic reel, because a wooden one will be too heavy for your parachute.

4 Hold the parachute so that the canopy is open and the thread reel dangles down. Stand by an upstairs window, or use a step-ladder to get as high as you can – but be very careful!

Let your parachute go from as high up as possible. As it falls, the canopy will open and fill with air. The larger the canopy, the slower the parachute will fall.

Ballooning around

YOU WILL NEED

pencil, cardboard, ruler, scissors,

sheets of tissue paper,

glue stick, hair dryer.

1 To make a template, draw a petal shape on cardboard and carefully cut it out. The shape should be 30cm/12in long and 12cm/4½in across with a flat bottom edge.

2 Draw around your template on seven pieces of coloured tissue paper. Be very careful not to rip the tissue paper with the tip of your pencil.

3 Use the pair of scissors to carefully cut out the shapes you have drawn. You should now have seven petals that are all the same size and shape.

To fly your balloon, hold its neck open and fill the inside with hot air from a hair dryer. After ten seconds, switch off the hair dryer and let go of your balloon to launch it into the air.

4 Glue along one edge of a petal. Lay another petal on top, and press it down. Open it out and stick on another petal in the same way. Keep going until the balloon is complete.

Streamlined design

Think of a sleek canoe moving through the water. Its streamlined shape hardly makes any ripples as it passes. Streamlined shapes also move easily through the air. They have low drag (air resistance). Angular shapes have more drag than rounded ones. The shape of a fast-moving fish has to be very streamlined. A fish such as a tuna has a blunt front end, is broadest about a third of the way along, then tapers towards the tail. This creates less drag as it moves through water than a shape with a pointed front end that broadens at the back. Water flows along each side of the tuna to rejoin without creating turbulence. The "Shape race" gives you a chance to design and test your own streamlined shapes.

Just as things that are moving in the air experience drag, so do stationary objects in the wind. Kites, such as the one here, are held up in the air by drag from the wind. For more than 3,000 years, people have been making and flying kites. The essential, but simple, secret is that it must be as light as possible for its size, so that it catches as much wind as possible. The kite design shown in this project has been used for many hundreds of years. Try flying it first of all in a steady wind, and experiment with the position of the bridle and the length of the tail.

YOU WILL NEED

pen, ruler, two bamboo canes (one about two-thirds as long as the other), string, scissors, adhesive tape, sheet of thin fabric or plastic, fabric glue, coloured paper.

▲ How air flows work
Air flows in gentle curves around the streamlined shape (*top*). Angles and sharp curves break up the flow and increase drag (*bottom*).

star

teardrop

square

▲ Shape race
Make different shapes (as shown above) from balls of modelling material that are exactly the same size. Race your shapes in water – the most streamlined shape should reach the bottom first.

Make a kite

1 To make the frame, mark the middle of the short cane and mark one-third of the way up the long cane. Tie the canes together crosswise at the marks with string.

2 Tape string around the ends of the canes and secure it at the top. This will stop the canes from moving, and it will also support the edges of your finished kite.

3 Lay the frame on top of the sheet of fabric or plastic. Cut around it, 2cm/¾in away from the kite's edge. This will give you enough to fold over the string outline.

4 Fold each edge of the material over the frame, and stick the edges down firmly with fabric glue (or adhesive tape if you are making the kite from plastic). Let the glue dry.

5 Tie a piece of string to the long cane, as shown – this is called the bridle. Tie the end of the ball of string to the middle of the bridle to make the tether.

6 Fold sheets of paper in zigzags. Tie them at about 25cm/10in intervals along a piece of string that is about twice as long as the kite. Glue or tie the tail to the bottom tip of the kite.

bridle

tail

tether

tassel

Now your kite is ready to fly! With the wind blowing on your back, reel out about 10m/10yds of tether. Ask an adult to gently launch the kite into the air. If it is not very windy, run into the breeze, pulling the kite to get it airborne. Now that you have built this kite, try experimenting with other materials and shapes, to find out which ones work well.

Curve and lift

Birds, gliders and airplanes all have wings. Their wings can be all sorts of different shapes and sizes, but they all have the same aerofoil (airfoil) design. This means that the top side of the wing is more curved than the underside. The aerofoil shape provides lift when air moves over it. Air flows faster over the curved upper surface than over the flatter lower surface. This reduces the air pressure above the wing, and lets the higher air pressure underneath lift it up.

You can make and test a model aerofoil by following the instructions in these projects. In the frisbee project, the shape of the frisbee allows the air to move smoothly over and under it. The frisbee spins as it flies. The spinning motion helps to steady it. The second project shows you how moving air, in this case, from an electric fan or hair dryer, can lift the wings with an aerofoil shape upwards.

Fly a frisbee

1 Place the plate face down on the cardboard, and draw around it with a pencil. Cut out the circle of cardboard. Draw slots 1.5cm/¾ in deep around the edge and cut these, as shown.

2 The cut slots around the edge will make tabs. Bend the tabs down slightly. Overlap them a little and stick them together with small pieces of adhesive tape.

Fly your frisbee outside, away from people. Hold it at the front and spin it away from you and up. It should glide through the air smoothly as the air pressure above it is reduced. Play toss-and-catch games with your friends. You could even have your own championship match! Commercial frisbees were introduced into the USA in the 1950s.

Aerofoil (airfoil) antics

1 Use a ruler to measure a rectangle of paper about 15cm/6in wide and 20cm/8in long. Use scissors to carefully cut out the shape. This will be your wing.

2 Fold the paper over, approximately in half. Use tape to fix the top edge 1cm/½in away from the bottom edge. Take care not to crease the paper as you do this.

3 Cut out and stick on a small paper fin near the rear edge of your wing, as shown. This will keep the wing facing into the airflow when you test it.

4 With a sharp pencil, carefully poke a hole through the top and bottom of your wing, near the front edge. Push a straw through the holes and glue it in place in the middle.

Hold the thread tight, and ask a friend to blow air from a fan or hair dryer over the wing. Watch it take off! This happens because the shape decreases the air pressure above the wing.

5 Cut a 1m/1yd-long piece of thick thread and thread it through the straw. Make sure that the thread can slide easily through the straw and does not catch.

Jet propulsion

A jet engine produces thrust from a roaring jet of super-hot gas. Its construction looks complicated, but the way it works is very simple. A powerful jet of gas moving in one direction produces thrust in the other direction. Imagine you are standing on a skateboard and squirting a powerful hose forwards. Jet propulsion will push you backwards. This reaction has been known for nearly 2,000 years, but it was not until the 1930s that it was applied to an engine.

In the first experiment, you can make a jet zoom along a string. The jet engine is like a balloon that produces thrust from escaping air. The second project demonstrates how a turbine works. Hot air produced by the gas jet turns the blades of the turbine. The turbine drives the fan at the front of the jet engine. These projects may seem simple, but they use the same scientific principles that propel all jet airplanes through the air.

Balloon jet

I Blow up the balloon and, while a friend holds the neck, tape the straw to its top. Thread the string through the straw and, holding it level, tie it to something to keep it in place.

▲ **Practical plane**
This passenger plane has four engines, two on each wing. Jet engines have revolutionized international travel. These planes carry millions of passengers around the world every year.

2 Let go of the neck of the balloon. A stream of air jets backwards and produces thrust. This propels the balloon forwards along the string at high speed.

Turbine lights

1 Using scissors, cut out the bottom of a large foil pie pan as evenly as possible. Make a small hole in the middle of the pan with the point of the compass.

2 Mark a smaller circle in the middle. Use a protractor to mark 16 equal sections of 22.5 degrees, and cut along each one to the inner circle. Use one scissor to cut along each line, if possible.

3 Angle the blades by holding the inner tip and twisting the outer edges 20 to 30 degrees. The middle of the inner tip should be flat, in line with the middle of the disc.

◄ Jet engine
The huge blades at the front of a jet engine suck in air and compress it. Fuel burns in the air to produce jets of hot air that blast from the rear of the engine, producing thrust.

4 Tape the blunt end of the pin to one end of the dowel. Finish it off neatly and trim if necessary. Place the bead on the pin. This will allow the finished turbine to spin freely.

Place the hole in the middle of the turbine over the pin. Ask an adult to light the candles. Hot air will spin the blades.

5 Put the dowel in the reel and press the reel into the modelling material in the middle of the plate. Place the candles on the plate around the reel.

Propeller flight

Propellers work in two different ways. When a propeller spins, it makes air move past it. Propeller-driven aircraft use this effect to produce thrust. Moving air also causes the propeller to spin. The projects here look at propellers working in these two ways. In the first one, you can make a simple paper propeller called a spinner. As the spinner falls, moving air rushes past the blades, making it revolve. This acts just like the fruits and seeds of maple and sycamore trees, which have twin propeller blades. As they drop from the tree, they spin and catch the wind, and are carried far away.

▲ Lift off

An aerofoil's (airfoil's) curved shape causes the air to flow faster over its upper surface than its lower surface. This reduces pressure from above and causes lift.

In the second project, you can make a spinning propeller fly upwards through the air. The propeller-like blades are set at an angle, like the blades of a fan. They whirl around and make air move. The moving air produces thrust and lifts the propeller upwards. Children first flew propellers like these 600 years ago in China.

In a spin

I Take a piece of paper, 15 x 9cm/ 6 x 3¾in, and draw a T-shape on it, as shown in the picture above. With a pair of scissors, cut along the two long lines of the T.

2 Fold one side strip forwards and one backwards, as shown above, making two blades and a stalk. Attach a paper clip to the bottom. Open the blades flat.

3 Drop the spinner and watch what happens. Before dropping it again, try giving each blade a twist to make your spinner spin around even faster.

Let's twist

I With the compasses, draw a circle 10cm/4in across on the card. Draw a circle 4cm/1½in across in the middle. With the protractor, draw lines dividing the circle into 16 equal sections.

2 Carefully cut out the circle and along the lines to the smaller circle. Twist the blades sideways a little. Try to give each blade the same amount of twist, about 20 or 30 degrees.

3 Make a hole in the middle of the cork slice with a bradawl. Put glue on the end of the dowel, and push it into the hole. Glue the cork to the middle of the propeller.

4 When the glue has dried, wind a long piece of string around the dowel. Drop the dowel into the thread reel launcher. You are now ready for a test flight.

Pull steadily on the string to move the propeller around. As the end of the string comes off, the blades produce enough thrust to lift the spinning propeller out of the launcher and into the air.

Model planes

Although a model is much smaller than a real full-size aircraft, it flies in exactly the same way. The control surfaces on the wings and the tail of a model plane or real aircraft work by changing the way in which air flows over the aircraft. This allows the pilot to steer the aircraft in different directions. Working together, the rudder and movable flaps called ailerons on the rear edge of each wing make the plane turn to the left or right. Moving flaps called elevators on the tail make the nose of the plane go up or down.

The scientific rules of flying are the same for any aircraft, from an airliner weighing 350 tons to this model made from paper, adhesive tape and a drinking straw. Making this model plane allows you to see how control surfaces, such as the aileron, rudder and elevators, work. The flight of any plane is very sensitive to the angle of the controls. They need to be only a slight angle from their flat position to make the plane turn. Too big an angle will make the model unstable.

▲ How to fly a plane

To turn the aircraft (yaw), the pilot turns the rudder to one side. To make the aircraft descend or climb (pitch), the pilot adjusts the elevators on the tailplane. To roll (tilt or bank) the aircraft to the left or right, the ailerons are raised on one wing and lowered on the other.

Glide along

YOU WILL NEED
pencil, set square, ruler, paper, scissors, glue stick, adhesive tape, drinking straw, paper clips or non-hardening modelling material.

1 Draw two rectangles, 22 x 10cm/ 8¾ x 4in and 20 x 3.5cm/8 x 1¼in. Mark ailerons 6 x 1cm/2½ x ½in on two corners of the larger one. Cut out two elevators 3.5 x 1cm/1½ x ½in on the other.

2 To make the wings, wrap the larger rectangle over a pencil and glue along the edges. Remove the pencil and make cuts along the 1cm/½in lines to allow the ailerons to move.

3 To make the tail, fold the smaller rectangle in half twice to form a W. Glue its middle to make the fin. Cut along the two 1cm/½in lines. Make a 1cm/½in cut on the fin to make a rudder.

4 Use adhesive tape to fix the wings and tail to the drinking straw (the plane's fuselage, or body). Position the wings about one quarter of the way along the straw.

5 Try adjusting the control surfaces. Bend the elevators on the tail slightly up. This will make the plane climb as it flies. Bend the elevators down to make it dive.

6 Bend the left-hand aileron up and the right-hand aileron down the same amount. Bend the rudder to the left. This will make the plane turn to the left as it flies.

Launch your plane by throwing it steadily straight ahead. To make it fly even farther, use paper clips or modelling material to weight the nose.

7 Bend the right-hand aileron up and the left-hand aileron down. Bend the rudder to the right slightly and the plane will turn to the right. Can you make it fly in a circle?

Escaping from Earth

The function of a space rocket is to carry a satellite or astronauts into Space. To do this, it has to overcome gravity (the force that pulls everything down to Earth). If a rocket's engines are not powerful enough, gravity will win and pull the rocket back to Earth. With more powerful engines, the rocket's attempt to fly into Space is exactly equalled by the pull of gravity. With these two forces in perfect balance, a spacecraft will continue to circle the Earth. If the rocket is even more powerful, it can fly fast enough to escape from Earth's gravity altogether and head toward the Moon and the planets. The speed that it needs to reach to do this is called escape velocity. You can see this in action by trying an experiment using a magnet and ball-bearings. You can also try launching your own cork model rocket from a plastic bottle.

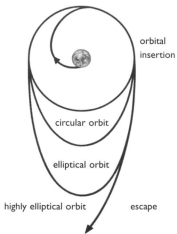

orbital insertion

circular orbit

elliptical orbit

highly elliptical orbit   escape

▲ Escape velocity

To go into orbit around the Earth, a spacecraft must reach a velocity of at least 28,500km/h/17,500mph. Depending on how fast it is travelling, the spacecraft may go into a circular, elliptical, or highly elliptical orbit. If it reaches a velocity of 40,200km/h/25,000mph, the spacecraft escapes from the Earth's gravity.

Launch a rocket

1 Place a teaspoon of bicarbonate of soda directly in the middle of a 10 x 20cm/4 x 8in piece of kitchen paper. Roll up the paper and twist the ends to keep the soda fuel inside.

2 Pour half a cup of water and the same of vinegar into the bottle. Fix paper streamers or a ribbon to the the cork with a pin. Drop the kitchen paper inside the bottle.

3 Push the cork in immediately so that it is a snug fit, but not too tight. Quickly take the bottle outside. Then move at least 3m/3yd away from it and watch what happens.

A chemical reaction between the vinegar (representing liquid oxygen) and bicarbonate of soda (baking soda) (representing fuel) produces carbon dioxide gas. The gas pressure inside the bottle pushes against the cork. The cork is blasted into the air like a rocket lifting off. However, in a real rocket, the gas is jetted out of the actual spacecraft, propelling it forwards.

Escaping from gravity

1 Measure out a 30 x 10cm/12 x 4in strip of thin card using a ruler. Cut it out with the scissors. Fold it lengthwise into four sections to form an M-shaped trough.

2 Cut the magnetic strip into five short pieces. Glue these short strips to the plastic base, so that they form a large, square bar magnet, as shown above.

3 Fix the magnet firmly to one end of the tray with some of the modelling material. Position it roughly in the middle. The magnet simulates the pull of the Earth's gravity.

4 Position one end of the trough over the edge of the magnet. Attach it to the magnet with tape. The trough represents the path of a rocket as it ascends into orbit.

5 Roll the remaining modelling material into a round ball. Position the ball underneath the other end of the M-shaped trough. This raises the trough at a slight angle.

6 At the end of the trough, place a ball-bearing and let it roll down. It sticks to the magnet. The ball-bearing's velocity along the trough isn't fast enough to escape the magnet's pull.

Raise the trough and roll another ball-bearing along it. The steeper angle increases the ball-bearing's velocity. Keep raising the trough and rolling ball-bearings, until one shoots past the magnet. It has then achieved escape velocity!

Rocket launch

Space rockets rely on jet propulsion to fly. When the rocket burns its fuel, a stream of hot gases roars out from the tail end and the rocket surges forwards. Jets flying lower than 25,000/82,000ft can burn their fuel using oxygen from the air. Space rockets need to carry oxygen with them, because above 25,000/82,000ft, the air thins and there is not enough oxygen.

Deep in the sea, octopuses also rely on jet propulsion to escape from their enemies. They squirt out a jet of water and shoot off in the opposite direction.

This experiment shows you how to make and fly a rocket that uses jet propulsion. The thrust of a rocket depends on the mass of propellant that it shoots out every second. Water is a much better propellant than hot gas, because it is so much heavier.

Follow these instructions carefully and your rocket could fly about 25m/80ft above the ground. You may need adult to help make some parts of this rocket and to launch it. When you are ready for a test flight, set your rocket up in an open space, well away from trees and buildings. This rocket is very powerful – you must not stand over it while it is being launched. Wear clothes that you do not mind getting very wet!

oxygen

hydrogen

combustion chamber

▲ **Inside a rocket**
This is a liquid-powered rocket. It carries liquid oxygen to burn its fuel (liquid hydrogen). The hydrogen and oxygen are pumped into the combustion chamber. The hydrogen burns furiously in the oxygen. The exhaust produces immense thrust.

Make a rocket

YOU WILL NEED
thin white card, pen, ruler, thin coloured card, scissors, plastic bottle, strong adhesive tape, funnel, jug (pitcher) of water, cork, bradawl, air valve, plastic tube, bicycle pump.

I Rockets have fins to make them fly straight. Draw out this fin template (it is about 20cm/8in long) on plain card and use it to cut out four fins from coloured card.

2 Decorate your bottle to look like a rocket. Fold the tab at the top of each fin. Use long pieces of strong tape to attach the fins to the bottle firmly.

3 Use the jug and funnel to half-fill the bottle with water. (The water is the propellant. Compressed air above the water will provide the energy that makes the thrust.)

4 Use the bradawl to drill a hole carefully through the cork. Push the wide end of the air valve into the plastic tube. Push the valve through the hole in the cork.

5 Hold the bottle with one hand, and push the cork and the valve into the neck of the bottle using the other hand. Push it in firmly so that the cork does not slide out too easily.

6 Attach the other end of the plastic tube to the bicycle pump. Turn your rocket the right way up – you are now ready to launch your rocket outside.

Look for a launch site far away from trees and buildings. Stand the rocket on its tail fins, and tell everyone to stand well back. Start pumping. Bubbles of air will rise up through the water. When the pressure in the bottle gets high enough, the cork and the water will be forced out and the rocket will fly upwards. Be careful not to stand over the bottle!

Going to the Moon

Plotting a course through Space is more complicated than traveling over land. Pilots follow natural features, such as hills, valleys and rivers; at high altitudes, they use radio beacons on the ground or satellite signals. The problem with journeying from the Earth to the Moon is that both are moving, as the first project illustrates. The second project shows how a heavy craft gets to the Moon. Staged rockets release their sections as they progress into Space, so reducing the weight of the rocket.

If a spacecraft was aimed straight at the Moon when it set off from Earth, the Moon would have moved on around its orbit by the time the craft arrived. If the spacecraft corrected its direction to follow the Moon's orbit, it would use too much fuel. Spacecraft are therefore aimed at the position the Moon will be in by the time the craft arrives. They navigate by the stars.

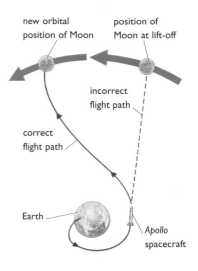

new orbital position of Moon

position of Moon at lift-off

incorrect flight path

correct flight path

Earth

Apollo spacecraft

▲ **Moving targets**
This diagram shows two possible flight paths for an *Apollo* spacecraft. Aiming directly at the Moon does not allow for its movement as it orbits the Earth. The correct, efficient route compensates for the Moon's orbital movements by aiming ahead of its position at lift-off.

YOU WILL NEED

Moving target: string, ruler, scissors, masking tape, metal washer, book, small balls of paper.
Two-stage rocket: two paper or plastic cups, scissors, long balloon and pump, adhesive tape, round balloon.

Moving target

1 Measure 2m/2ft of string with the ruler. Cut it off with scissors. Tape one end of the string to one end of the ruler. Tie a washer to the other end of the string.

2 Place the ruler on a table or box, with the string hanging over the edge. Weight it down with a heavy book. Try hitting the washer by throwing small balls of paper at it.

3 Start the washer swinging, and try to hit it again with the paper balls. See how much more difficult it is to hit a moving target, like a spacecraft aiming at the moving Moon.

third stage powers command/service module (CSM) toward the Moon

second stage fires

second stage jettisoned

third stage fires

first stage jettisoned

▲ Rocket staging

The *Saturn 5* rocket had three stages. The first two powered the spacecraft up through the atmosphere. The third stage propelled it into orbit, and then gave an extra push to send the craft on its way to the Moon.

Two-stage rocket

1 Using scissors, carefully cut the bottoms out of the paper or plastic cups. These will serve as the linking collar between the two stages of the balloon rocket.

2 Partly blow up the long balloon with the pump. Pull the neck of the balloon through the paper or plastic cups. This balloon will be your two-stage rocket's second stage.

3 Fold the neck of the long balloon over the side of the cups. Tape the end of the neck of the balloon to the cups to stop the air from escaping, as shown.

4 Carefully push the round balloon into the open end of the paper or plastic cups, as shown. This balloon will form the first stage of your two-stage balloon rocket.

5 Blow up the round balloon, so that it wedges the neck of the long balloon in place inside the cups. Hold the neck of the round balloon to keep the air inside it.

Peel the tape off the neck of the long balloon. Hold the rocket as shown. Let go of the round balloon's neck. Air rushes out, launching the first stage of the rocket. It then falls away, launching the second-stage balloon.

Artificial gravity

Space voyagers in orbit far away from Earth do not feel the pull of gravity. They feel weightless, as if they are forever falling. In a state of weightlessness, there is no up or down, because up and down are created by the force known as gravity. Even experienced pilots and astronauts sometimes feel uncomfortable and ill until they get used to being weightless. Weightlessness also has damaging effects on the human body. Future space stations and spacecraft designed for very long spaceflights may create artificial gravity to protect their occupants from the effects of weightlessness.

Make a centrifuge

In this project, you can explore a theoretical method of creating artificial gravity that uses rotation by making a centrifuge. Moving objects tend to travel in straight lines. When you whirl around a ball attached to the end of a piece of string, it tries to fly off in a straight line, stopped only by the string. Inside a rotating spacecraft, the solid outer walls would stop astronauts flying off in straight lines. This would feel like the astronauts were being pushed down to the ground, just like the effect of gravity on Earth.

YOU WILL NEED

four cardboard triangles (30 × 10 × 22.5cm/12 × 4 × 8¾in), dishwashing detergent bottle, adhesive tape, bradawl, wooden skewer, long rubber band, masking tape, three paper clips, pliers, cardboard strip (50 × 5cm/20 × 2in), small bead, scissors, drinking straw, two small plastic cups, non-hardening modelling material, water, food dye.

1 Take the four cardboard triangles and tape them to the sides of the bottle, as shown. These will provide the dishwashing detergent centrifuge with a broad, stable base to stand on.

2 Using the bradawl, make a hole in the bottom of the detergent bottle. Push one end of the rubber band almost all the way into the hole using a wooden skewer.

3 Pass the wooden skewer through the small loop of rubber band projecting from the hole, as shown. Leave an equal amount of skewer on either side of the bottle.

4 Take the masking tape and firmly secure the wooden skewer to the base of the detergent bottle. Make sure that the skewer is fixed so tightly that it cannot move.

5 Straighten out one end of a paper clip with pliers. Dip the hooked end of the clip into the neck of the bottle. Catch the rubber band with the hook and pull it out.

6 Using the bradawl, make a hole in the middle of the cardboard strip. Thread the end of the hooked paper clip through the bead. Then thread it through the hole in the cardboard.

7 Carefully bend the end of the paper clip down on to the cardboard strip. Using the adhesive tape, fix the end of the clip securely into place, as shown above.

8 Use the scissors to cut two short pieces of drinking straw. Each piece should measure 5cm/2in in length. Fix one piece to each end of the cardboard strip with the tape.

9 Take one of the small plastic cups. Carefully make a hole with the scissors on both sides of the cup near the top. Now make holes in the second cup in the same way.

Stick the centrifuge to a flat surface with modelling material. Fill the cups one-quarter full with water. Add food dye to make the water show up clearly. Then turn the cardboard strip until the rubber band is wound up. Let the strip go, and watch the cups as they spin around rapidly. The cups fly outward, but the water is held in place by bases of the cups.

10 Straighten two paper clips with pliers. Thread a clip through each straw. Bend the ends of the clips into hooks using pliers. Thread the ends of the clips through the holes in the cups.

Working in Space

There is no gravity outside the pressurized crew compartment of a shuttle in Space. This makes work more difficult than on Earth. On Earth, gravity pulls us down to the ground. We can then use friction against the ground in order to move around. If a weightless astronaut pushes a handle in zero gravity, he or she would fly away in the opposite direction! This means that astronauts have to be anchored to something solid before doing any work. A spacesuit makes it even more difficult to move. The astronaut has to push against the suit to close a hand, or bend an arm or leg.

Spacesuit gloves have thin rubber fingerpacks, so that astronauts can feel things through them, but their sense of touch is still very limited. The first project

▲ **Working in a spacesuit**
Bulky spacesuits make working in space difficult. Spacesuit designers are always trying to improve them. The more flexible a suit is, the less tiring it is to work in. This means that an astronaut can work outside for longer periods, a great help when they are making repairs.

simulates the experience of working in a spacesuit by using rubber gloves, a bowl of water and some nuts and bolts. Then make a robot arm like the shuttle's remote manipulator system (RMS), which is used to launch and retrieve satellites.

Nuts and bolts

1 Take the nuts and bolts, and place them on a table. Now try picking them up and screwing them together. You should find this a very easy task to achieve!

2 Now try screwing the nuts and bolts together with the gloves on. This is more difficult, like trying to perform a delicate task on Earth wearing bulky spacesuit gloves.

3 Fill the bowl with water. Add the nuts and bolts. Try screwing them together with the gloves on. This is very difficult, like working in a spacesuit outside a spacecraft.

Make a robot arm

1 Use the ruler to measure three 28 x 5cm/11 x 2in cardboard strips. Cut them out. Use a bradawl to make a hole 2.5cm/1in from the ends of each strip. Join the strips with split pins.

2 Take the hook and screw it into the end of the dowel. The dowel will be used to control the robot arm remotely, just as shuttle astronauts remotely operate the RMS.

3 Now carefully bend one of the paper clips into the shape of the letter S. To attach the paper clip, pass it through the hole in the end of the cardboard arm, as shown.

Pass the hook on the dowel through the hole in the end of the cardboard arm. Move the dowel to operate the robot arm remotely. Try to pick up the ball using the S-shaped paper clip.

4 Take the modelling material and roll it into a ball about the size of a walnut. Then take the second paper clip and push it firmly into the ball, as shown.

Glossary

A

aerodynamics The way in which objects move through the air.

aileron A moving flap on the trailing (rear) edge of an aircraft wing.

air pressure The force with which air presses on things. Changes in air pressure makes air move, and causes different weather conditions.

aerofoil (airfoil) An object, shaped like a wing, that creates lift in the air.

alloy A material, usually a metal, such as bronze or brass, that is made from a mixture of other materials.

aperture A hole behind the lens of a camera, which can be adjusted to let more or less light on to the film.

APS (Advanced Photographic System) A camera that allows you to change the format for individual shots.

artificial Describes something that is not created as part of a natural process or with naturally occuring materials.

atmosphere The layer of air that surrounds a planet and is held to it by the planet's gravity.

atom The smallest part of an element that can exist. It is made up of many other smaller particles including electrons, neutrons and protons.

autofocus A feature on a camera that automatically adjusts the lens position to make sure that a scene is in focus.

B

bacteria A simple living organism, usually consisting of a single cell. Many bacteria are parasites and cause disease.

battery A container of chemicals that holds a charge of electricity.

binary code The digital code computers use, made up of two numbers, "0" and "1".

bow The front end of a ship.

brake A pad or disc that slows a moving surface down by pressing it.

brake van A carriage at the back of trains used in the mid-1800s. A guard riding in the brake van applied the brakes following instructions from the driver in the locomotive.

C

CAD Computer-aided design.

camouflage The adoption of tones, patterns and texture in order to merge with the environment and so be hidden or disguised.

camshaft A device that creates a regular, rocking movement, such as the opening and shutting of a valve on a car cylinder head.

carbon dioxide A colourless, odourless gas containing the elements carbon and oxygen, which is a part of air.

cargo Goods carried in a ship or other vehicle.

caterpillar The larva of a butterfly or moth.

CD-ROM (compact disc read-only memory) A portable computer disc, similar to an audio CD, that stores information.

chemical A substance used by scientists, in industry and at home.

chemical reaction The process by which one or more substances react together and change into one or more different chemicals.

chlorophyll The green pigment of plants that absorbs light energy from the Sun.

climate The typical weather pattern of an area.

cocoon A silky, protective envelope, such as that secreted by silkworms and other insect larvae, to protect the developing pupa.

compass An instrument that contains a magnetized strip of metal, used for finding direction.

compressed air Air that has been squashed into a smaller volume than usual.

condensation The process by which water vapour becomes a liquid.

conductor A material through which heat or electricity can travel.

continental drift The generally accepted theory that continents move slowly around the world.

continental shelf The zone of shallow water in the oceans around the edge of continents.

convection The rising of hot air or fluid, caused by the fact that it is lighter than its surroundings.

counterweight A weight that balances another weight.

coupling A connecting device that joins a locomotive to a carriage to make a train.

coupling rod A link that connects the driving wheels on both sides of a locomotive.

crankshaft An axle that has parts of it bent at right angles so that up-and-down motion can be turned into circular motion.

crystal A mineral or other substance that forms in a regular, 3-dimensional shape.

cylinder A hollow or solid tube shape.

D

data Pieces of information.

database An organized store of information.

deciduous Describes trees and shrubs that shed their leaves at the end of each growing season.

density A measure of how tightly the matter in a substance is packed together.

deposition The laying down of material, particularly of material eroded from the Earth's crust and carried by rivers, sea, and ice.

depth of field In photography, the

distance in focus between the nearest and farthest parts of a scene.

digital camera A camera that takes electronic images that are downloaded onto a computer to be viewed.

dish antenna A large, dish-shaped aerial used to receive signals in radar, radio telescopes, and satellite broadcasting.

disc drive The device that holds, reads, and writes on to a disc.

drag A force that acts in the opposite direction to motion and creates resistance.

driving wheel The wheel of a locomotive that turns in response to power from the steam engine.

E

Earth's crust The outermost, solid rock layer of the planet Earth.

ecosystem A community of living things that interact with each other and their surroundings.

effort The force applied to a lever or other simple machine to move a load.

electricity A form of energy caused by the movement of electrons (charged particles) in atoms.

element A substance that cannot be split by chemical processes into simpler parts.

elevator In aircraft, a movable flap on the tailplane or rear wing that causes the nose to rise and fall.

engine A device that uses energy in fuel to make movement.

environment The external conditions in which people, animals, and plants live on Earth.

epicentre The region on the Earth's surface that lies directly above the focus of an earthquake.

Equator The imaginary circle around the middle of the Earth, between the Northern and Southern Hemispheres,

where day and night are equal in length, and the climate is constantly hot and wet.

erosion The gradual wearing away of the land by agents of erosion such as ice, rain, wind and waves.

escape velocity The minimum speed that a body must have to escape from the gravitational force of a planet.

evaporation The process by which something turns from liquid to vapour.

evergreen Describes plants that bear leaves all the year round.

exoskeleton Outer skeleton – the hard case that protects an insect's soft body parts.

exposure time The time it takes for a camera to take a picture.

exposures Photographs on a film.

F

fault A break in the Earth's crust that causes one block of rock to slip against an adjacent one.

fax machine A machine that photocopies and electronically sends and receives written words and pictures over a telephone line.

fertilization The act or process of the male part of a plant, or a male animal, that allows a female's seed, egg or eggs to produce young.

focal plane The area at the back of a camera where the exposed film is held flat.

force A push or a pull.

fossil The remains, found preserved in rock, of a creature that lived in the past.

freight Goods transported by rail, road, sea and air.

friction The force caused by the two surfaces rubbing together. This results in the slowing down of movement and heat being produced.

fumarole An opening in the ground in volcanic regions, where steam and gases can escape.

G

gauge The width between the inside running edges of the rails of a train track. In Britain, the USA and most of Europe, the gauge is 1,435mm/4ft 8½in.

gear A toothed wheel designed to interact with other toothed wheels to transfer motion in a controlled way.

generate To produce energy such as electricity.

geology The scientific study of the origins and structure of a planet and its rocks.

geothermal energy The energy created by the heat of the rocks underground.

germination The point at which a plant seed, or an egg in an animal, is fertilized and begins to grow.

geyser A fountain of steam and water that spurts out of a vent in the ground in volcanic regions.

gravity The pulling force that exists between large masses.

H

hard disc A computer's main storage disc, which holds the operating system and application files.

hardware All the equipment that makes up a computer – disc drives, monitor, keyboard, mouse etc.

hemispheres The top and bottom halves of the Earth, divided by the Equator, and known as the Northern and Southern Hemispheres.

hibernation A period when many animals save energy by remaining inactive in order to survive the winter.

hot spot A place where plumes of molten rock in the Earth's mantle burn through the Earth's crust to create isolated areas of volcanic activity.

hot springs Water that has been heated underground and bubbles to the surface in volcanic regions.

hull The frame or body of a ship or aircraft.

humidity The amount of water, or moisture, in the air.

hydraulics The use of water and other liquids to move devices such as pistons.

hydrometer An instrument for measuring the density of liquids.

hygrometer An instrument for measuring humidity.

I

igneous rock A rock that forms when magma (hot, molten rock) cools and becomes solid. It is one of three main types of rock, the others being sedimentary and metamorphic rock.

infrared Electromagnetic radiation with a wavelength between the red end of the visible spectrum, and microwaves and radio waves.

insulate To cover or protect something to reduce the amount of heat or electricity entering and/or leaving it.

J

jet engine a type of engine that propels a vehicle, such as a car or a plane, by the forceful expulsion of hot gases.

jet propulsion Reactive movement to a jet of fluid or gas.

K

keystone The central stone in the arch of a bridge or curved part of a building.

L

larva The immature stage in the life of many insects, amphibians and fish.

lava Hot, molten rock emerging through volcanoes, known as magma when underground.

leading wheel The wheel at the front of a locomotive.

lens A transparent object, such as glass, that is curved on one or both sides. A lens bends and directs beams of light to form or alter the view of an image.

lever A long bar that moves around a pivot to help move a heavy object.

lift The force generated by an aerofoil (airfoil) that counters the force of gravity and keeps a flying object in the air.

light spectrum The colours that light can be split into.

lithosphere The rigid outer shell of the Earth, including the crust and the rigid upper part of the mantle.

load The weight moved by a lever or other machine.

locomotive An engine powered by steam, diesel or electricity, and used to pull the carriages of a train.

M

magma Hot, molten rock in the Earth's interior, known as lava when it emerges on the surface.

magnetism An invisible force found in some elements but especially in iron, which causes other pieces of iron to be either pushed apart or drawn together.

mantle The very deep layer of rock that lies underneath the Earth's crust.

mass The amount of matter there is in a substance or object. Mass is measured in kilograms, pounds, tons, etc.

metamorphic rock Rock that has been chemically changed by heat and pressure to form a different rock.

metamorphosis Change, as in the life cycles of some animals, that involve a complete change of form, appearance, and other characteristics.

meteorologist A person who studies the science and patterns of weather and climate.

mineral A naturally occurring substance that is found in rocks.

mould A kind of fungus in the form of a woolly growth that is often found on stale and rotten food.

molten Something solid that has been melted, such as lava, which is molten rock.

monochrome Shades of black and white, with no other colours.

monorail A train that runs on a single rail.

mummy An embalmed or preserved body.

N

navigation The skill of plotting a route for a ship, aircraft or other vehicle.

negative In photography, the image on the developed film from which photographic prints are made. The colours in a negative are reversed, so that dark areas appear to be light and light areas appear to be dark.

O

orbit In astronomy, the curved path followed by a planet or other body, around another planet or body.

order A major grouping of animals, larger than a family.

organism Any living thing, such as a plant or animal, that is capable of growth and reproducing itself.

osmosis The movement of a solvent, such as water, from a more dilute solution to a more concentrated one.

P

palaeontology The study of fossils.

photosynthesis The process by which plants make food using energy from sunlight.

piston A cylindrical device that moves up and down a cylinder, in response to the application and release of pressure from liquid or gas.

pivot A central point around which something revolves, balances or sways.

plastic A durable, synthetic material that is easily shaped by heat.

plumb line A string with a weight at one end that is used to check whether a building is vertical.

points Rails on the track that guide the

wheels of a locomotive onto a different section of track.

precipitation Any form of water (rain, hail, sleet and snow) that comes out of the air and falls to the ground.

primary colours Red, blue and green, or magenta, cyan (blue) and yellow. These are the basis for all other shades and colours.

prism Specially shaped glass used to split white light into the spectrum, and to refract light rays away from their normal path.

propellant The fuel or force that causes something to go forward, such as the fuel in a rocket.

propeller A device, with blades, that rotate to provide thrust for a vehicle, such as a ship or plane.

prototype The first working model of a machine from a specific design.

pupa Inactive stage in the life cycle of many insects, such as butterflies and moths.

R
RAM (random access memory) Computer memory that holds data temporarily until the computer is switched off.

reflecting telescope A telescope that uses mirrors.

refracting telescope A telescope that uses lenses.

refraction The bending of light rays.

rolling stock The locomotives, carriages, wagons and any other vehicles that operate on a railroad.

ROM (read-only memory) Computer memory that holds information permanently.

rudder A device for controlling the direction of a ship or plane.

S
satellite A celestial or artificial body that orbits around a planet or star.

savanna Tropical grassland.

sediment Solid particles of rock or other material.

sedimentary rock A rock that is made up of mineral particles that have been carried by wind and running water to accumulate in layers elsewhere, most commonly on the beds of lakes or in the seas and oceans.

seismology The study of earthquakes.

shutter Camera mechanism that controls the amount of time light is allowed to fall on the lens.

software Applications that allow computers to carry out specific tasks.

Solar system The family of planets, moons and other bodies that orbit around the Sun.

solution A mixture of something solid and the liquid into which it has been completely dissolved.

sound wave Energy that transmits sound.

space probe A spacecraft that works in deep space.

space shuttle A vehicle designed to be used for at least 100 space flights.

space station A large, artificial satellite in which astronauts live and work.

species A group of animals that share similar characteristics and can breed successfully together.

steam traction Pulling movement achieved through the conversion of water to steam.

streamlined A shape that moves through air or water in the most efficient manner, with the least resistance from drag or friction.

T
tectonic plates The 20 or so giant slabs of rock that make up the Earth's surface.

tectonics The study of the structures that make up the Earth's surface.

thermometer An instrument for measuring temperature.

thorax The part of an insect's body between the head and the abdomen, which bears the wings and legs.

thrust The force that pushes something, such as an aircraft or ship, forwards.

tidal wave A huge ocean wave.

transpiration The process in the water cycle by which plants release water vapour into the air.

tropical A climate that is very hot and humid.

tropics Part of the Earth's surface that is between the Tropic of Cancer and the Tropic of Capricorn.

turbine A propeller-like device that is driven by fast-moving gas currents, wind and water.

turbulence Air or water movement that consists of eddies in random directions, with no smooth flow.

U
upthrust The force that makes a ship float or an aircraft take off.

V
valve A device that controls the flow of a liquid.

W
waterwheel A simple, water-driven turbine used to drive machinery.

weather The condition of the atmosphere at any particular time and place.

weathering The breakdown of rock and other materials when they are exposed to the weather.

weightlessness In Space, a state in which an object has no actual weight, because it is not affected by gravitational attraction.

wind Air moving in relation to the Earth's surface.

windmill A machine for grinding and pumping, driven by vanes or sails that are moved by the wind.

Index

A

acid test, for minerals 66–7
acorn, germinate an 81
ailerons 236–7
air pumps 154–5
aircraft
    jet engines 232
    model planes 236–7
    propeller-driven 234
aerofoils (airfoils) 230–1
albatrosses, giant 114
ammonites 62
Andes 40
andesite 58
animals
    cold-blooded 100
    tracks and footprints 96–7
    see also birds; insects
antiseptic cream 135
ants 112–13
apertures 178, 179
apple seeds 88
aquariums 94, 95
Atlantic Ocean, mid-ocean ridge 30
atoms, in crystals 56
avocado pits 89

B

balance scales 148, 149
balloons 226, 227
barchans 26
bark, tree 74, 76–7, 79
basalt 58
binary code 164
binoculars 116
bird cake 122, 123
bird tables 123
birdbaths 118
birds 114
    body shape 114
    diving 114, 115
    drawing 114, 115
    feathers 124–5
    feeding 122–3
    listening to 118–19
    migration 126, 160
    nests 120–1

telltale traces 124–5
travel and flight 126–7
watching 116–17
black smokers 45
boats and ships
    cargo 198, 199
    floating 194–5
    hulls 194, 195, 196–7, 198, 199
    power and steering 200–1
    safety measures 202–3
    sailboats 192–3
    self-righting boats 202
    simple boats 190–1
    stability 198–9
body, levers 146
brakes, car 220–1
bread 132
    decay 135
bridges 140
    arch 138, 139, 140
    beam 140
    building 138–9
    platform 138
    suspension 140
buds, tree 78
buoyancy tanks 202, 204
butterflies see moths and butterflies

C

cameras 176
    apertures 178, 179
    film 174
    and light 172–3
    pinhole 176–7, 178
    shutters 178
    single lens reflex 176, 177
camshafts 220, 221
can crushers 148
carbon dioxide 131, 238
    and plants 80
    in volcanoes 46, 47, 50, 51
carburettor 220
cars
    assembly 222
    brakes 220–1
    camshaft 220, 221
    carburettor 220

development 224
engines 216
gears 218
keeping cool 222–3
making a model car 224–5
making the wheels turn 216–17
casts, footprint 97
catamarans 198
caterpillars 108, 110–11
cathode ray tubes 170
cement, natural 61
centrifuge, making a 244–5
chemical change 130–1
clouds 22, 23, 81
coastlines 18–19
colours, secondary 170, 171
compasses 158, 159
    loop 161
computer-aided design 224
computer data storage 164–5
comsats 183
concrete 136, 137
condensation 22
cones, tree 78, 79
conglomerates 60, 61
conifers 78
continents
        crustal plates 38
        movement 30, 31
coracles 190, 191
core, Earth's 42
crankshafts 216, 218
crystals, making 56–7
currents, ocean 16, 17

D

decay 134
    prevention 135
    see also decomposition
decomposition (decay), in soil 72–3
deltas 20, 21
density, of rocks or minerals 66, 67
digital images 170
dish antennae see radio dishes
domains, magnetic 156
drag 226, 228
dunes, sand 26

E

Earth
  crustal plates *see* tectonic plates
  layers 42
  light reaching 10
  magnetism 158–9
  night and day 10
  satellites 182–3
  seasons 10, 11
  see also earthquakes; rocks; volcanoes
earthquakes 30, 32–3
  causes 38
  epicentre 32
  focus 32
  measuring 34–5, 36–7
earthworms 70
ecosystems 94–5
electric motors 150, 151
electrolysis 130, 131
electromagnetism 162–3
  Olympics using 168, 169
energy
  creating 150–1
  from liquid and air 154–5
engines
  car 216
  jet 232, 233
epicentre 32
epiphytes 82–3
ergs 26
erosion, by water 20–1
escape velocity 238, 239
evaporation 81
exoskeletons 100
experiments, hints 7

F

fan belts 222–3
faults 38, 39
  volcanoes along 42
fax machines 170
feathers 124–5
films, camera 174
fishing, magnetic 166, 167
flight
  bird 126–7
  insect 98

  propelled 234–5
flowers 102
  on trees 79
food chains or webs 94
footprints, animal 96–7
forests
  building a shelter 90, 91
  conifer 90
  life in 90
  reproducing plant conditions in a bottle 92, 93
  temperate 78, 90
  tropical rainforests 74, 78, 90, 92
  vanishing 92
  see also trees
fossils 62–3
frisbees 230
fruits 88–9
fumaroles 52

G

gases
  atoms in 56
  in volcanoes 46, 47, 50–1, 54, 55
gears 218–19
geodes 64
geothermal features 52–3
germination, seeds 80, 81
geysers 52, 53
gorges, river 20
Grand Canyon 61
granite 54, 58, 59
gravimeters 34
gravity
  artificial 244–5
  escaping from 239
  zero 246, 247
gravity boost 184
Great Pyramid, in Egypt 136
grippers 148, 149

H

heat, and chemical change 130, 131
hides, bird 116–17
Himalayas 40
hot spots 42
hot springs 52

hovercraft 202, 203
hulls 196–7, 198, 199
  hollow 194, 195
humidity 24–5
hydraulic machines 154
hydrocarbons 130
hydrofoils 202, 203
hydrometers 194
hydroplanes 204
hygrometers 24, 28

I

imprints, fossil 62, 63
insects 100
  camouflage 104, 105
  drawing 100, 101
  flight 98
  food samples for 106
  inside 100
  pollination by 102
  at ponds 106, 107
  searching for 98–9, 106–7
  surveys 100, 101
  vision 102
  see also ants; moths and butterflies
intrusions, igneous 54, 55
iron filings, and magnets 156
islands 42

J

jet propulsion 232–3, 240–1

K

Kilauea (volcano) 49
kites 228, 229

L

lava 46, 58
  viscosity 48, 49
leaf insects 104
leaves
  tree 78, 79
  veins 82
lenses, and telescopes 180, 181
level, surveyor's 145
levers 146–7
  experiments with 148–9

lifeboats 202
lifting
    using hydraulic machines 154
    using levers 147
light
    and cameras 172–3
    images from 170–1
lightning 150
liquids 56
logging 92
loudspeakers 162
Love waves 33

M
magma 42, 43, 44–5, 52, 54, 55, 58
magnetism
    and computer data storage 164, 165
    Earth's 158–9
    electric magnets 162–3
    fun with magnets 166–9
    how magnets work 156–7
    magnetic fields 158, 159, 162
    and maps 160–1
magnetosphere 158
mantle, Earth's 42, 44
maps
    and magnets 160–1
    weather 28
marble 54
mazes 161
mechanical advantage 146
metamorphosis, complete 110
mid-ocean ridge 30
migration, bird 126, 160
minerals 64
    specific gravity 67
    testing for 66–7
mini-jungle 92, 93
mirrors, and telescopes 180
Mohs' scale 64, 65
Moon
    face of the 12
    going to the 242–3
    phases 12–13, 14
    and tides 14, 15
moths and butterflies 108–9
    butterfly garden 108, 109
    caterpillars 108, 110–11

motors, electric 150, 151
mountains, formation 30, 38, 39, 40–1
mud holes (mud pools) 52, 53
mummification 134

N
nesting boxes 121
nets, pond 107
Newton's cradle 34
night and day 10
nutcrackers 146, 148
nuts 89

O
obsidian 58, 59
ocean waves and currents 16–17, 18
oil, formation 130
Old Faithful 52
Olympics, electromagnetic 168, 169
orbits, types 182
osmosis 84–5
owls 118
    pellets 125
oxygen, from plants 80

P
palaeontology 62
Pangaea 30
panpipes 186, 187
paper, photographic 174
parachutes 226
pellets, bird 124, 125
photograms 174, 175
photographic images 174–5, 178
photosynthesis 80, 82
pitfall traps 98–9
plants
    for butterflies 108, 109
    growth 80–1
    insect pollination 102
    and light 82–3
    surveys of 86
    and water 24, 80, 81, 84–5
    window boxes 104, 105
    see also epiphytes; fruits; trees
plastic flow 44
plumb lines 144
pollination, by insects 102

Pompeii 51
pools, for insects 106, 107
pooters 98, 99
preservation and decay 134–5
probes, space 184, 185
propellers
    in air 234–5
    underwater 200, 201
pumice 54, 58
pupae 108
pyramids 136, 142–3

R
racing, magnetic 168
radio dishes 182, 184, 185
radio waves, and satellites 183
rain 22
    forecasting 28
    measuring rainfall 23, 28
rainbows 172
rain gauges 22, 23, 28
Rayleigh waves 33
reed boats 190
ripples, in sand 19
rivers 20
robot arm, making a 247
rockets 238, 239, 240–1
    staging 243
    two-stage 243
rocks 66
    conglomerate 60, 61
    hardness 64, 65, 67
    igneous 54, 56, 58, 67
    intrusive 54
    metamorphic 54, 67
    sedimentary 54, 60–1, 67
    and soil 70
    specific gravity 66, 67
    testing 64–7
    volcanic 54
roots 92
rudders 200, 201

S
sailboats 192–3
St. Helens, Mount 44, 50
San Andreas Fault 32
San Francisco 32

sand
  dunes 26
  ripples in 19
  sorted by wind 26
satellites 182–3
savanna 78, 90
scales, balance 148, 149
sea mounts 42
seasons 10, 11
seeds 86, 88, 89
  dispersal 86, 87
  germination 80, 81
seesaws 146, 147
seifs 26
seismographs 36–7
shape race 228
shelter, building a 90, 91
ships *see* boats and ships
slingshot effect 184
soil 70–1
  decomposers in 72–3
  erosion 92–3
  horizons 70
solids 56
sound 186–7
  waves 186, 187
sound reflectors 119
Space, working in 246–7
spacecraft 238–9, 240
  artificial gravity 244
  space probes 184, 185
  to the Moon 242, 243
spacesuits 246
specific gravity, of rocks
  or minerals 67
spoons, as levers 146
sports, magnet 168–9
stick insects 104, 105
stone and concrete 136–7
strata 60, 61
streak test 65
streamlining 228–9
submarines 204–5
sugar
  crystals 56
  representing magma
    58, 59
Sun, and Earth 10, 11

surveying 144–5
swamps, mangrove 80
switches 163

T
tectonic plates (crustal plates) 30
  floating 38
  forming mountains 39, 40
telephones 162
telescopes 180–1
televisions 163, 170
temperature changes, measuring 24–5
thermometer, making a 10, 11
tides 14–15
tiltmeters 34, 35
tipis 117
tracks, animal 96–7
transpiration 22, 84, 85
trees 74
  bark 74, 76–7, 79
  deciduous 74
  germinating an acorn 81
  girth 75
  growth rings 29, 75
  height 75
  identification 74, 75
  insects on 102, 103
  measuring the crown 77
  roots 84
  specimens from 78–9
  see also forests
tree trap, making a 103
tremors, Earth 32
tunnels 140–1
turbines 150, 232, 233
  wind 152
tweezers 148

U
upthrust 194, 195

V
vacuum cleaners 154, 155
valleys, rift 39
velocity, escape 238, 239
viewer, making a 172, 173
vision
  insect 102

  of a woodcock 114
volcanoes 30, 42, 44
  chains 42
  erupting 46–7, 54
  gases inside 46, 47, 50–1, 54, 55
  hot spots 42
  shapes 48–9
  undersea 48
  see also lava

W
water
  cycle 22
  density measured 194
  and plants 24, 80, 81, 84–5
  shaping the landscape 20–1
  vapour 22, 80, 81
  see also humidity
water wheels 152, 153
waves
  earthquake 32, 33, 34
  making 19
  ocean 16–17, 18
  sound 186, 187
weather
  humidity 24–5
  measuring rainfall
    22, 23
  recording 28–9
  wind 26–7, 28
weather vanes 26, 27, 28
weathering 70
weightlessness 244, 246
wind 26–7, 28
wind turbines 152
windmills 27, 152
window boxes 104, 105
wings
  aerofoil (airfoil) 230
  bird 127
wood, weather recorded in
  growth rings 29
woodcocks, vision 114
woodlice 72
wormery 70, 71

Y
yeast 132–3

Acknowledgements

This edition is published by Hermes House, an imprint of Anness Publishing Ltd, 108 Great Russell Street, London WC1B 3NA; info@anness.com

www.hermeshouse.com; www.annesspublishing.com

If you like the images in this book and would like to investigate using them for publishing, promotions or advertising, please visit our website www.practicalpictures.com for more information.

© Anness Publishing Limited 2014

A CIP catalogue record for this book is available from the British Library.

Publisher Joanna Lorenz
Project Editor and Picture Researcher Rasha Elsaeed
Consultant Chris Oxlade
Contributing Authors Stephen Bennington, John Farndon, Ian Graham, Jen Green, Peter Harrison, Robin Kerrod, Peter Mellett, Al Morrison, Chris Oxlade, Steve Parker, John Roston, Rodney Walshaw
Contributing Editors Gilly Cameron Cooper, Rebecca Clunes, Louisa Somerville, Joy Wotton
Designer Sandra Marques/Axis Design Editions Ltd
Jacket Design Jonathan Davison
Photographers Paul Bricknell, John Freeman, Don Last, Tim Ridley
Nature Photographer Robert Pickett
Illustrators Cy Baker/Wildlife Art, Stephen Bennington, Peter Bull Art Studio, Stuart Carter, Simon Gurr, Richard Hawke, Nick Hawken, Michael Lamb, Alan Male/Linden Artists, Guy Smith, Clive Spong, Stephen Sweet/Simon Girling and Associates, Alisa Tingley, John Whetton
Stylists Ken Campbell, Jane Coney, Marion Elliot, Tim Grabham, Thomasina Smith, Isolde Sommerfeldt, Melanie Williams
The publishers would like to thank all the children modelling in this book.

PUBLISHER'S NOTE
Although the advice and information in this book are believed to be accurate and true at the time of going to press, neither the authors nor the publisher can accept any legal responsibility or liability for any errors or omissions that may have been made nor for any inaccuracies nor for any loss, harm or injury that comes about from following instructions or advice in this book.

Manufacturer: Anness Publishing Ltd, 108 Great Russell Street, London WC1B 3NA, England
For Product Tracking go to: www.annesspublishing.com/tracking
Batch: 7422-23432-0004

Picture Credits
b=bottom, t=top, c=centre, l=left, r=right
Bruce Coleman Ltd: 87cl. Frank Lane Picture Agency: 87bl, 96bl, 96bc, 96br. Nature Photographers Ltd: 76bc